# PRAISE FOR "RISING OF THE THOROUGHBREDS"

*Having seen the distance and the disparity between prophets and pastors firsthand, this manuscript has been written in the perfect timing of God. We are living in an age where men and women of God lack the clarity necessary to move beyond their current circumstances and rise above mediocre expectations. This young apostle to the prophets has penned a book that finally addresses the most urgent issues the Church is currently facing in light of a generation of "Elishas that have no Elijahs." Through the revelation in this book, pastors and prophets can finally truly join forces and experience unparalleled unity. Its effect on the world and the Body of Christ can be matchless. This is God's original intent—for the prophets to rise up and decree the vision of the purposes of our God, within the context of the local church and the world. This book will help transform how you see your destiny and will accelerate its manifestation in this last day move of the Spirit.*

**~Bishop Charles Martin,
All Nations Champions Church, Oklahoma City, OK**

*Prophet John Coleman is dedicated to preserving the integrity of the prophetic ministry and mantle. His diligent search of the Scriptures and devotion to spending quality time in the presence of God is evident in his accurate delivery of the Word of God.*

*In his new book entitled "Rising of the Thoroughbreds," John gives insight into prophetic balance and in his own* words, he helps you to "simplify it and not just amplify it." I love horses, so the title drew me in immediately, but it was the revelational content that keeps me reading page after page. This is a great book for both those who are veterans in the field of the prophetic as well as those who are new to this notable call.

*~Bishop Alvernis L. Johnson,*
*Kingdom Life Ministries International, Founder,*
*Saginaw, MI*

"Rising of the Thoroughbreds," by Deland John Coleman, is a breath of fresh air for all believers. As a proven prophetic voice, he skillfully articulates the heart of God for prophetic ministry. We believe this is a much-needed resource because, unfortunately, the ministry of the prophet has been mishandled, undervalued, and underappreciated in the Body of Christ. "Rising of the Thoroughbreds" paints a clear picture for why we must all operate prophetically but also how to do it with integrity and wisdom. We believe every believer needs to read this book, as it will be life-changing!

*~LaJun & Valora Cole,*
*LaJun and Valora Cole Ministries, Perfected Love International Fellowship, Senior Servants, Bestselling Authors of "Sudden Breakthrough"*

"Rising of the Thoroughbreds" is one of the most practical and beneficial books written on prophetic character, disciplines, training, and order. The unfolding of prophetic insight will challenge and serve seasoned prophets as well as assist in the development of new and budding prophets. Well done, Prophet John.

*~Apostle Cynthia Chess,*
*Mountain's Hope Community Worship Center,*
*Tracey, CA*

"Rising of the Thoroughbreds" will challenge you in unexpected ways, yet draw you into the authenticity of the heart of Prophetic ministry through the confirmation of the Word of God. Written with the purpose of bringing about clarity with understanding so that the reader is well versed and advanced in prophetic ministry, Deland John Coleman has established an identity of authentic prophets and prophetic ministry. With the challenge will come the knowledge, and thankfully "Rising of the Thoroughbreds" will also equip many for the advancement of the Kingdom.

~Ryan Johnson,
Ryan Johnson Ministries, Fort Payne, AL

Had an opportunity to look over a few of the chapters briefly. It reads personal and simplistic, with Scripture references, and I really look for that. Your own testimonies really bring home your compassion and strong conviction of your revelation as it pertains to the prophetic. Can't wait to see the finished product.

~Pastor Vincent L. Walker,
Right Way Christian Center, Mobile, AL

It's not often that a human gets his purpose and God's timing right. This is an example of just that. After reading and combing through specific ideas in this book I have to say I am edified. The writing is compelling, yet easy to understand. I look forward to the testimonies that will come from people reading and applying these solid principles. This book is an actual testament of what can happen when a person carries a high view of God's Word as well as practice of right theology. I ask anyone looking for something that will stretch them mentally and spiritually to get this book and never let it go.

~Bishop Stan Williams,
The Church 320, Jacksonville, FL

# RISING OF THE THOROUGHBREDS:

A GUIDE TO FINDING BALANCE IN PROPHETIC MINISTRY

D. JOHN COLEMAN

Rising of the Thoroughbreds:
A Guide to Finding Balance in Prophetic Ministry
by D. John Coleman

Cover design, editing, book layout and publishing services by KishKnows, Inc., Richton Park, Illinois, 708-252-DOIT
admin@kishknows.com, www.kishknows.com

ISBN 978-1-7325756-0-8
LCCN 2018908289

All rights reserved. No part of this book may be reproduced, distributed, or transmitted in any form or by any means, including photocopying, recording, digital scanning, or other electronic or mechanical methods, without the prior written permission of the publisher, except in the case of brief quotations embodied in critical reviews and certain other noncommercial uses permitted by copyright law.

For permission requests, please contact: D. John Coleman at pastorjdcoleman@sbcglobal.net

Some Scripture references may be paraphrased versions or illustrative references of the author. Unless otherwise specified, all other references are from the **King James Version of the Bible.**

Scriptures taken from **THE HOLY BIBLE, NEW INTERNATIONAL VERSION®, NIV® Copyright © 1973, 1978, 1984, 2011 by Biblica, Inc.®** have been used by permission. All rights reserved worldwide.

Scripture quotations taken from the **Amplified® Bible** (AMP), Copyright © 2015 by The Lockman Foundation Used by permission. www.lockman.org

Unless otherwise noted, all quotations are attributed to the author. All rights reserved.

Copyright © 2018 by D. John Coleman

Printed in the United States of America

# DEDICATION

To my amazing family: Kisia, Kennedy, Christian, Ca'Koia, Rain, and Jream.

To our Kingdom Church International family… to all of my Obadiah mentee's, (past and present) … to all of my boot camp students, Classes 101 and 102… to all of the pastors and leaders who have poured into my life from near and far, and finally… to all of the prophets of God who are evolving and forming into the mouthpiece of God… continue to pursue your purpose in the prophetic. Every last one of you continues to stretch me and keep me focused.

**Thank you.**

# CONTENTS

Foreword ............................................................................. 1
Introduction ...................................................................... 3

**Chapter 1**
Prophetic Balance ........................................................... 7

**Chapter 2**
Prophetic Default or Prophetic Design? ................... 13

**Chapter 3**
Prophetic Gap ................................................................ 17

**Chapter 4**
Missing It ........................................................................ 33

**Chapter 5**
Sensitivity ....................................................................... 45

**Chapter 6**
Organic vs. Artificial Prophetic Ministry ................... 57

**Chapter 7**
Prophets and Profits .................................................... 63

**Chapter 8**
The Thread of the Prophetic ...................................... 83

**Chapter 9**
Understanding the Mantle ......................................... 89

**Chapter 10**
The "Three P's" of the Prophetic ............................... 93

**Chapter 11**
The Burden of the Prophetic .................................... 101

**Chapter 12**
Thoroughbreds and Black Stallions ........................ 113

## Chapter 13
The Right Prophetic Company .................................................. **125**
Conclusion .................................................................................... **135**
Prophetic Charges and Decrees ............................................ **137**
A Prayer Over the Prophets
and the Prophetic Ministry Gifts ............................................ **143**
## Appendix
References to Prophecy in the Scriptures ....................... **145**
About the Author ..................................................................... **149**
Contact the Author .................................................................. **151**
Testimonials ............................................................................... **153**

# FOREWORD

In this season of the Church, we can't afford to desire the status quo of man-made laws and principles of an organization. This is an "Issachar Season," of a Body of Christ coming forth in the mantles designed for each believer, dipped in the blood of Jesus for His purposes and designs. This book, "Rising of the Thoroughbreds" by Dr. John Coleman, has been birthed to train those of us who believe there's a greater outpouring to come upon God's Army of Believers. We will mount up and go forth in His power and demonstration, without fear of mankind, or the cost.

This book is destined to awaken us to the full measure of the blueprints written in the scrolls of Heaven concerning "the Gifts of the Holy Spirit." 'Greater things will we do,' was prophesied by Jesus to those called by His name. We truly believe Jesus showed us all the greater things while He walked upon the Earth, but He knew our Father would turn up the grid of power in these last days, for His children to do greater exploits! Why? To show Himself strong for all the world to see!

We recommend this book for all those who know their calling in the office of a prophet, and to those that are just stepping into their callings. This book will train you, and equip you to hear the voice of God, and always be obedient to the promptings of the Holy Spirit.

As Prophet John wrote this book by the inspiration of the Holy Ghost, for the believers to 'Mount Up,' take your position as a trained thoroughbred, waiting to be released for such a time as this! Go with God's power, His fire, and His Glory!

*Drs. Frank & Karen Sumrall*
*Sumrall Global Ministry*
*www.sumrallministry.com*

# INTRODUCTION

*True prophets do not express their opinions! They express the **absolute**s from the Word of God.*

*The prophetic grants me **exceptional** life and **extraordinary** life, and allows me to experience an **epic** life in God. God desires for His people to live in advancement and abundance.*

"As a pregnant woman about to give birth writhes and cries out in her pain, so were we in your presence, LORD. We were with child, we writhed in labor, but we gave birth to wind. We have not brought salvation to the earth, and the people of the world have not come to life. But your dead will live, LORD; their bodies will rise—let those who dwell in the dust wake up and shout for joy—your dew is like the dew of the morning; the earth will give birth to her dead." Isaiah 26:17-19 (NIV)

"Arise, shine, for your light has come, and the glory of the LORD rises upon you. See, darkness covers the earth and thick darkness is over the peoples, but the LORD rises upon you and his glory appears over you. Nations will come to your light, and kings to the brightness of your dawn." Isaiah 60:1-3 (NIV)

I want to personally take this opportunity to thank you for taking the time to read my book, and to invite you into my heart and spirit as we journey on this prophetic quest together.

I know for a fact that if you will just listen with your inner ear and discern the voice of the Lord, this book will equip you, empower you, and challenge you to go to the next level in the prophetic.

I was stirred late last year as the Spirit of God really began to deal with me on the subject of prophetic balance. One morning, as I was in devotion, I heard the Holy Spirit say, "John, in this season, I will raise you up as an apostle to prophets!" I had never heard of such a thing, to be perfectly honest. However, I *knew* it was the voice of God. Later, as I was ministering out-of-town, my host began to prophesy the Word of the Lord over my life concerning things which nobody knew of but God. It was indeed 100% clarification and confirmation.

I have been involved in the prophetic ministry for over two decades... more than half of that in the office of the prophet. I was so stirred after hosting my first conference here in Illinois. The Hand of the Lord was all over it. The opposition was severe and the warfare was intense. However, God got the glory, and lives were impacted and activated into their prophetic destiny. The Lord supernaturally had one person write a check and pay for the entire cost of the conference! Glory to God! When you step out in the *vision* God, will supply the *provision*.

*How amazing is that?*

In this book, we will be addressing somethings that have been ignored and overlooked in the prophetic ministry. For instance, when did it become more important to choose...

- **gifts** over **fruit?**
- **wrong** over **right?**
- **disorder** over **order?**
- **title** over **tenure?**

**"Therefore, my brothers and sisters, be eager to prophesy, and do not forbid speaking in tongues. But everything should be done in a fitting and orderly way." 1 Corinthians 14:39-40 (NIV)**

I believe that we are in a season in the Church where we need the prophetic with *depth*. Not your "hanging on the wall" degrees... we need more *training*. Not "opportunities." We need more *presence* than *presentation* and more of the *Word* than of your "*intellect*." It doesn't impress God at all!

The word *order* here is defined as "a standard of living which places your life on a definable track and makes life less complicated by eliminating confusion." Bishop I.V. Hilliard, author of *Wisdom Insight,* says, "When it all comes down to the wire, 'confusion' is simply the breeding ground for disorder and chaos." Boom, **Boom**, and **BOOM**!

It is my sincere desire that as you read this book, you will gain greater insight into the subject of prophetic balance. So please... grab some Starbucks, Dunkin Donuts or whatever your preference is. Sit back, open up, and prepare to mount up as we set the stage for *Rising of the Thoroughbreds.*

*"One of the reasons the prophetic is so misunderstood is because we should know how to **simplify** it, instead of always trying to **amplify** it. Start practical and **qualify** it, so that **wisdom is present.**"*

*Chapter 1*

# PROPHETIC BALANCE

"A false balance is abomination to the LORD: but a just weight is his delight." Proverbs 11:1 (KJV)

*"Real prophets are determined by their fruit, not their gifts! The church is in trouble when the gifts become more important than the fruit."*

**"Now about the gifts of the Spirit, brothers and sisters, I do not want you to be uninformed. You know that when you were pagans, somehow or other you were influenced and led astray to mute idols. Therefore, I want you to know that no one who is speaking by the Spirit of God says, "Jesus be cursed," and no one can say, "Jesus is Lord," except by the Holy Spirit. There are different kinds of gifts, but the same Spirit distributes them. There are different kinds of service, but the same Lord. There are different kinds of working, but in all of them and in everyone it is the same God at work. Now to each one the manifestation of the Spirit is given for the common good. To one there is given through the Spirit a message of wisdom, to another a message of knowledge by means of the same Spirit, to another faith by the same Spirit, to another gifts of healing by that one Spirit, to another miraculous powers, to another prophecy, to another distinguishing between spirits, to another speaking in different kinds of tongues, and to still another the interpretation of tongues. All these are the work of one and the same Spirit, and he distributes them to each one, just as he determines." 1 Corinthians 12:1-11 (NIV)**

**"Follow the way of love and eagerly desire gifts of the Spirit, especially prophecy. For anyone who speaks in a [tongue] does not speak to people but to God. Indeed, no one understands them; they utter mysteries by the Spirit. But the one who prophesies speaks to people for their strengthening, encouraging and comfort. Anyone who speaks in a tongue edifies themselves, but the one who prophesies edifies the church. I would like every one of you to speak in tongues, but I would rather have you prophesy. The one who prophesies is greater than the one who speaks in tongues, unless someone interprets, so that the church may be edified." 1 Corinthians 14:1-5 (NIV)**

*"God often raises up prophets to deal with that which is **Relevant** and that which is **Prevalent**."*

*"Prophets are led and fed by the Spirit of God, and not moved, influenced or controlled by religion or a man."*

It is imperative to note that the prophetic has attached to it what I call "Prophetic Parameters." For so long, we have been a church society that loves to flow in the gifts; however, gifts alone, without order, *will not suffice.* **Gifts without character produce chaos!**

Unfortunately, the church has been built under false pretenses, such as raising offerings under the spirit of manipulation, ordaining people who really were not ready, or perhaps even giving prophetic words out of the timing and the season of the Lord.

Ironically, when it comes to the prophetic in some of our churches, it's "leaning for lack of learning." We are high in one area and deficient in another. There is a statement that I have coined... *"When I discern, I learn."* Simple and straight to the point.

When acrobats want to attempt walking on the high ropes, they don't just walk out there! They invest the time to train their bodies and condition themselves to be able to balance when they're in the air, walking on the rope. Athletes go through training camps for the purpose of stretching their muscles to maximize their performance on the field. If they don't take the time to properly prepare, they risk cramping up and experiencing muscle discomfort. It's the same in ministry. What I'm trying to convey here is this: **Don't allow yourself to cramp your prophetic muscles!**

In order for prophecy to obtain optimum results, it's important to have prophetic conditioning and positioning. Just as athletes require regular conditioning to maintain their performance on the field, so it is with the gift of prophecy as it relates to the ministry gifts. Athletes who do not train regularly and take the time to keep their bodies in good condition will not achieve the results that their coaches are expecting, and will be in danger of causing the whole team to perform poorly. It is the same with the gift of prophecy. If we are not ready, but operate out of a place of immaturity and impatience, or are inconsiderate of our fellow Christians, we will "pollute the prophetic air," and do more harm than good.

**"Let all things be done decently and in order." 1 Corinthians 14:40 (KJV)**

The objective of *conditioning* is to get you set for *positioning*. I have seen many prophetic churches and people who have been given the gift of prophecy, but have not *invested* in their prophetic assignment.

When this happens, you risk continual misalignment. No sports team expects to be successful unless they know for sure that they have made the initial sacrifice to soar, and likewise, no prophetic church or individual will thrive in their gift unless they take the time to invest in their assignment.

**S:** No more **SETTLING**
**O:** Seize the right **OPPORTUNITY**
**A: ANSWER** the call to wealth
**R: REAP** from your efforts

As much as *you* think you may want to soar in your gift, be assured that *God* intends for you to go higher than you have ever dreamed. However, it will always require the *investment* before there's *influence* and the development of your gift in *private* before you want to go *public*. Let it occur in God's timing, not yours, and you'll be more successful in fulfilling your purpose.

**"For I know the thoughts that I think toward you, saith the Lord, thoughts of peace, and not of evil, to give you an expected end." Jeremiah 29:11 (KJV)**

I remember in high school, (when my legs were much younger) running cross country track and playing softball and basketball. My coaches would always say, "Coleman, if you want to last in the game, you've got to show up for practice!" I must admit that as an eager teenager, I had one thing on my mind and it definitely was not practice! I wanted to play in the games, but without the investment. I can remember the times when my stomach would cramp up, and I'd hear Coach saying, "You should have been in practice!" Boy, that's real talk there... and I did *not* want to hear it! But of course, as the season went on, I finally figured out why some of the other guys would stay later. They were *making the investment*.

Why am I sharing this little story, you might ask? Because it is so relative to the church, and to the prophetic ministry. We *want to do* what we *want to do,* without having to make the initial investment or sacrifice. There are some well-known prophetic churches and ministries that are unfortunately "lopsided" in the spirit. They may be calling themselves "prophets" or "prophetic ministries," but some of them are just so off, and you can't tell them anything. They are "strong in their wrong," and the character factor in their lives is absent. This is one reason why I believe that there is such a stirring in the purpose and understanding of the prophetic. I strongly sense that God is raising up "Apostolic Arrows" to assist us in our aim, so that we don't miss the mark and mess it up.

Remember the story of Elijah and Elisha? The protégé Elisha took the time to both sit with and travel with Elijah, and it wasn't so that he could be the one preaching. He just wanted to serve the man of God. Let me be honest here. This generation of prophetic ministry gifts has a spirit of entitlement and doesn't understand the patience factor that is necessary in the prophetic. It is a requirement for every prophetic gift to go through what I call the "Prophetic Phase Process." This is the place where your prophetic gift is developed, and you establish yourself with balance in the prophetic.

*"The prophetic, when unlearned and unskilled, is like film that is undeveloped—there is no clear picture."*

**Elijah is Taken to Heaven**

**"When they had crossed, Elijah said to Elisha, 'Tell me, what can I do for you before I am taken from you?'**

**'Let me inherit a double portion of your spirit,' Elisha replied.**

**'You have asked a difficult thing,' Elijah said, 'yet if you see me when I am taken from you, it will be yours—otherwise, it will not.' As they were walking along and talking together, suddenly a chariot of fire and horses of fire appeared and separated the two of them, and Elijah went up to heaven in a whirlwind. Elisha saw this and cried out, 'My father! My father! The chariots and**

horsemen of Israel!' And Elisha saw him no more. Then he took hold of his garment and tore it in two. Elisha then picked up Elijah's cloak that had fallen from him and went back and stood on the bank of the Jordan. He took the cloak that had fallen from Elijah and struck the water with it. 'Where now is the LORD, the God of Elijah?' he asked. When he struck the water, it divided to the right and to the left, and he crossed over. The company of the prophets from Jericho, who were watching, said, 'The spirit of Elijah is resting on Elisha.' And they went to meet him and bowed to the ground before him. 'Look,' they said, 'we your servants have fifty able men. Let them go and look for your master. Perhaps the Spirit of the LORD has picked him up and set him down on some mountain or in some valley.' 'No,' Elisha replied, 'do not send them.'" 2 Kings 2:9-16 (NIV)

"Consequently, you are no longer foreigners and strangers, but fellow citizens with God's people and also members of his household, built on the foundation of the apostles and prophets, with Christ Jesus himself as the chief cornerstone. In him the whole building is joined together and rises to become a holy temple in the Lord. And in him you too are being built together to become a dwelling in which God lives by his Spirit." Ephesians 2:19-22 (NIV)

"But the fruit of the Spirit is love, joy, peace, forbearance, kindness, goodness, faithfulness, gentleness and self-control. Against such things there is no law. Those who belong to Christ Jesus have crucified the flesh with its passions and desires. Since we live by the Spirit, let us keep in step with the Spirit. Let us not become conceited, provoking and envying each other." Galatians 5:22-26 (NIV)

*Chapter 2*

# PROPHETIC DEFAULT OR PROPHETIC DESIGN?

*"Just because God accepts your **gift** doesn't mean He approves of **you**."*

## Operating in "Default Mode"

Many people today are operating in the prophetic by "default" instead of by "design." The reason is that when you see the things that often occur in the prophetic ministry, you can really begin to question, and ask yourself, "Is this really the plan of God? Is this really my time to move out? Has that person really been called to the office of the prophet?"

These, and so many other questions, require authentic answers, but too often, believers become anxious or overzealous, and just want to walk in the office of a prophet or start a ministry, when it actually requires sacrifice, process, and a "God said" (inspired by the Holy Spirit) not a "good said" (something that *sounds* good... but may not be God's plan for your life!)

I have encountered quite a few prophetic ministry gifts who operate by default. This means no investment; no time spent in His presence or in the Word. This complacency traps them and leaves them in a mediocre place when it comes to their relationship with God. To live a life in God "by default" is simply just to *settle*. You sit down, stay in the struggle, and continue to serve the Lord, but act like it's a strain.

Look at it this way. If there is a sweepstakes, and you have a ticket, you can assume that others have one as well. Your winnings may not be the same as those of the other entrants. If the people who are awarding the prizes say, "We will give you a prize just for showing up," to me, that implies a "default." I don't know about you, but I want *everything* Daddy God has for me. I don't want a prophetic gift that just *exists*; I want a prophetic anointing with *fire* and *demonstration in the Holy Spirit*!

How do you know when your prophetic gift is "in default?"

- It's just "hanging on"
- God is not moving the way He's supposed to
- You find yourself saying, "I want to... but I can't"
- There's no passion and fire in your flow
- You depend on others to get your prophetic words to share with others

You get the picture, right? I know that there have been times in my life where I have chosen to operate in my gift by default, because I didn't have anyone to challenge me with my gift. I must say, the rewards now are so much greater when I see God use me to speak a word over someone's life or situation. It is priceless! If God can do it for me, He can do it for you, but you must *choose not to live in your prophetic gift by default!*

Your prophetic gift may *allow* you to be in the midst of several great men and women of God, but do not mistake the timing of the *delivery* for the timing to *use it*. You may be there just to learn and listen, and take in before you speak, because more than likely, their language is very different from yours.

**"Therefore, I glory in Christ Jesus in my service to God. I will not venture to speak of anything except**

**what Christ has accomplished through me in leading the Gentiles to obey God by what I have said and done by the power of signs and wonders, through the power of the Spirit of God. So, from Jerusalem all the way around to Illyricum, I have fully proclaimed the gospel of Christ. It has always been my ambition to preach the gospel where Christ was not known, so that I would not be building on someone else's foundation." Romans 15:17-20 (NIV)**

To continue to function in the prophetic by default will do more damage than good, and can cause harm to those who need to hear from the Lord, and in your own life as well.

### Operating by Design

Now, let's look into operating in the prophetic by "design." When something operates according to its original intent, it's an indication of design. For example, a house is designed to provide a covering or shelter, so that you and your family don't have to live outside. A car is designed to transport you from one location to another; a basketball is designed to go through a net on the court; a pair of shoes is designed for your feet, and so on.

The same principle can be applied to the prophetic gift. The prophetic was designed to confirm, to align, and to clarify; to awaken you, to activate you, to edify you, to equip you, exhort you, to comfort you, and ultimately, to establish you into your purpose.

The word **edify** means "to construct or to build up something or someone." **Exhort** is defined as "provoking to purpose, drawing you nearer to your destiny," and finally, **comfort** as it is used here means "to eliminate the clutter, the crazy, the chaos and the confusion, and release clarity and peace."

When the prophet operates by God's design, miracles occur, lives are blessed, and the church at large is empowered and equipped to pursue and recover.

## Chapter 3

# PROPHETIC GAP

*"When the **foundation** of the prophetic is cracked, it will often produce prophetic gifts who are not **balanced**."*

"Now the boy Samuel was attending to the service of the Lord under the supervision of Eli. The word of the Lord was rare and precious in those days; visions [that is, new revelations of divine truth] were not widespread. Yet it happened at that time, as Eli was lying down in his own place (now his eyesight had begun to grow dim and he could not see well) and the [oil] lamp of God had not yet gone out, and Samuel was lying down in the temple of the Lord, where the ark of God was, that the Lord called Samuel, and he answered, 'Here I am.' He ran to Eli and said, 'Here I am, for you called me.' But Eli said, 'I did not call you; lie down again.' So, he went and lay down. Then the Lord called yet again, 'Samuel!' So, Samuel got up and went to Eli and said, 'Here I am, for you called me.' But Eli answered, 'I did not call, my son; lie down again.' Now Samuel did not yet know [or personally experience] the Lord, and the word of the Lord was not yet revealed [directly] to him.

So the Lord called Samuel a third time. And he stood and went to Eli and said, "Here I am, for you did call me." Then Eli understood that it was the Lord [who was] calling the boy. So, Eli said to Samuel, 'Go, lie down, and it shall be that if He calls you, you shall say, "Speak, Lord, for Your servant is listening."' So, Samuel went and lay down in his place. Then the Lord came and stood and called as at the previous times, 'Samuel! Samuel!' Then Samuel answered, 'Speak, for Your servant is listening.' The Lord said to Samuel, 'Behold, I am about to do a thing in Israel at which both ears of everyone who hears it will ring. On that day, I will carry out against Eli everything that I have spoken concerning his house (family), from beginning to end. Now I have told him that I am about to judge his house forever for the sinful behavior which he knew [was happening], because his sons were bringing a curse on themselves [dishonoring and blaspheming God] and he did not rebuke them. Therefore, I have sworn to the house of Eli that the sinful behavior of Eli's house (family) shall not be atoned for by sacrifice or offering forever.' So, Samuel lay down until morning. Then he opened the doors of the Lord's house.

But Samuel was afraid to tell the vision to Eli. But Eli called Samuel and said, 'Samuel, my son.' And he answered, 'Here I am.' Then Eli said, 'What is it that He said to you? Please do not hide it from me. May God do the same to you, and more also, if you hide from me anything of all that He said to you.' So, Samuel told him everything, hiding nothing from him. And Eli said, 'It is the Lord; may He do what seems good to Him.' Now Samuel grew; and the Lord was with him and He let none of his words fail [to be fulfilled]. And all Israel from Dan [in the north] to Beersheba [in the south] knew that Samuel was appointed as a prophet of the Lord. And the Lord continued to appear in Shiloh, for the Lord revealed Himself to Samuel in Shiloh by the word of the Lord." 1 Samuel 3:1-21 (AMP)

Notice in this text how the Word of the Lord was not present. The Bible tells us that the Word of the Lord was rare and precious in those days; visions (new revelations of divine truth) were not widespread. There was a span of 400 years between the Old and New Testaments where there was no prophetic Word from the Lord. We see even here how there was a major gap in the prophetic. I can't even begin to fathom what state the Body of Christ today would be in without a prophetic word for 400 years. Churches wouldn't survive, marriages would fall apart, relationships wouldn't last, and businesses would fold without the intervention of the prophetic ministry. It is a scary thought when you consider it! No fire, no release, no glory, no strong worship. All of these are just merely platforms where the prophetic ministry can operate. The prophetic anointing unleashes an extraordinary wind of God's grace to carry you into your future.

Even in my own life, I have realized the impact and effect that the prophetic has had on me. It has literally *changed my life*. I'm sure many of you can relate to this statement. The prophetic grace has brought many of you to the place you are in God right now!

We see in the story with the prophet Samuel how the Lord began to call him and prepared him for his calling as a prophet in the Lord's army. God knew that there was a need to have a prophetic voice; a sound that echoes the sentiments of the Father. I love how the story begins to build, as Samuel begins to discover his prophetic assignment. As Samuel is confirmed as a young prophet with the call of God on his life, Eli begins to discern that this young man has been called by the Lord. As we look more into this text, I want us to see how relative this is to us today in our local church.

There are some churches that just don't understand the prophetic ministry. So now, we have prophetic gaps in our churches and church services. I can only imagine how some people are spiritually dying because there are no prophetic utterances permitted.

So many people are walking around incomplete, unfulfilled, unsatisfied, under a spell, or trapped by the spirit of

Jezebel. Of course, this spirit does *not* want the prophets to prophesy, or for the people to receive prophetic ministry! Its goal is that it wants all of the attention. Jezebel is in the form of anything that is not the authentic presence of God. (For reference, the story of Jezebel and Ahab is found in the Books of **First** and **Second Kings**).

When I think about it, the prophetic ministry is literally like the "second wind" that inflates the lungs so that you can breathe and take in your assignment in God. I believe that this aggressive spirit of distraction and disorder thrives on, hanging at the door of the prophetic. This spirit has been assigned to stand at many church doors in the spirit, to shut up the prophets and the prophetic voices. When this happens, these gaps are established.

These gaps are also formed by ignorance—people simply just not knowing. There are prophetic gaps in different areas and regions. You can enter some churches and know right away that there is a gap. Then there are other churches that will allow the prophetic with a "catch," which is still a form of control.

Let me share another story with you. I can remember what happened like it was yesterday. I began as the prophet Samuel had done, hearing things, and I wasn't sure why or how I was hearing them. I would be in a service and all of a sudden, the spirit of prophecy would come over me, and I wouldn't realize it at the time. Eventually, that grace came upon me and God began to show me things. Even in my own life, as a teenager that loved God, I knew that something greater than just a "religious experience" was out there. I felt God stretching me and raising me up, and during that season, there was no public prophetic display, no activations, and no words of knowledge or the gifts of the Spirit really in operation. I distinctly remember how the Lord dealt with me at one particular time. I began to inquire of Him, and I started visiting a prophetic ministry in the city of Chicago. Little did I know it would change my life forever!

There was a *prophetic seed* that was lying dormant in me, and it needed to be activated. This is one reason why I can appreciate others as well as myself traveling from city to city and state to state during prophetic boot camps and activations. There are so many churches and cities where there is a spiritual famine: no moisture, no dew on the ground, no saturation of worship, no moving in the gifts of the Spirit, and no spontaneity. It was like that during this particular time in my life. The prophetic pipes were stopped up with fear, religion, doubt, Jezebel, the spirit of Saul, and ignorance. Like David, I began to pursue the heart of God, and I developed a holy hunger for the gifts of the Spirit. It didn't matter that my friends and family didn't want to chase after this—I just knew in my heart that God was doing something different in my life.

I was the eldest child, and growing up in my neighborhood and home, going to church was "okay." But as many of you know, it is more than just going to church, being in the choir, and being part of the youth group. When I was growing up, you were considered crazy if you wanted God at such a young age, and people thought you were weird if you spent most of your time in church. Bottom line—something was wrong with you! I'm so glad I didn't let that season of my life become a tomb for me to stay in. I can honestly say that it pays to pursue your purpose!

**Music**

Even as a child, I was drawn to music. When I was young, I was molested by an older cousin. I really didn't understand what was going on, but I knew it didn't feel right. Music was there (I know now) to help suppress what was going on internally. There are so many people in our world today who have been violated by family members, and others that they trusted. As I got older, and really understood what had happened, I knew I had to forgive her. I made up my mind that I wasn't going to be one of those people who isolated themselves, and was unable to form healthy relationships. You would be surprised at the freedom that you will find, if you just learn to open up and talk about it. Unfortunately, life happens to us all, but when there is a relationship with the Father, it can make such a difference to a wounded soul, or the life of a wounded individual. I don't know who this may be for, but whoever it is, *you've got this*. What happened was *not your fault* and it is time to be free, in *Jesus' name*! I felt like I needed to share this to bless someone else. I didn't realize the impact that it had on my life until I was older.

People often wonder why I'm so passionate about worship. When you've gone through some of the things I've been through, including being homeless for a season of my life, you become very appreciative toward the things of the Lord. Sometimes, people can't believe some of my stories, but I assure you—these things did occur! There was even a young lady with whom I had gotten serious, and we were discussing marriage. One day, she invited me over to her home. (All guys know when a girl says, "We need to talk," you are instantly on guard!) To my surprise, she wanted to end the relationship, and go back to her baby girl's father. Was I devastated? Absolutely! For the first time in my life, the thought of suicide entered my mind.

I'll never forget how, after that conversation, I went home and sat in the bathtub, and it was as if the devil was on a loudspeaker in my head. "You fool! She didn't really love you anyway!" I entertained these words and others, and I found the longest knife I could find in the kitchen and took off my shirt with the intention of ending my life.

I did not realize that God was living on the inside of me; and when I lifted the knife into the air, a worship song by Israel Houghton fell in my spirit. I immediately came to myself and started worshipping God. I tell you all of this to say that worship saved me from suicide. To God be the glory!

**Suicide** is defined as "the act of taking one's own life, voluntarily and intentionally."

Here are seven instances of suicide in the Scriptures:

- **Abimelech: Judges 9:52-54.** Abimelech lacked personal identity.
- **Samson: Judges 16:25-30.** Samson died for a cause he believed in as well as for revenge.
- **Saul: 1 Samuel 31:4.** Saul was stressed, unable to live up to certain expectations, felt rejected, and felt as if he was a failure.
- **Saul's armor-bearer: 1 Samuel 31:5.** It was an impulsive act; he wanted to die with his master.
- **Ahithophel: 2 Samuel 17:23.** Ahithophel was bitter because his advice had not been followed.
- **Zimri: 1 Kings 16:15-20.** This was an act of rebellion; Zimri had a problem with authority.
- **Judas: Matthew 27:3-5.** Depressed, Judas felt trapped by materialism and guilt.

This is a spirit that has been increasing among our youth of today. Today, I declare in *Jesus' name* that the Spirit of the Lord will arise upon those who struggle with suicidal thoughts. I break off spirits of depression and rejection, and I declare an infusion of joy in the Holy Ghost right now, in *Jesus' name*. Be free, woman of God! Be free, man of God! Right now, in *Jesus' name*! I take authority over your emotions, and I call for order and balance in your life, right now, in *Jesus' name*!

I didn't always fit in with the crowd. I wasn't aggressive, was often quiet and shy, and kept to myself until I began to venture outside of my comfort zone. I have always had a love for music. It was my solace. It was an outlet, and it was just one of things that I loved. I would never in a million years have thought that I would be doing what I am right now. Not that I was a bad person; but I believe that God put the desire for music in me, and it grew until I was very passionate about it. Now, in hindsight, I see how the Lord was working behind the scenes.

One of things I've come to realize about the prophets of God and the prophetic is that the prophetic ministry is strongly influenced by worship and praise music. The Bible talks about praise and worship throughout the Scriptures. I have discovered that when there is an atmosphere created for God, He responds and releases *Rhema*, *Restoration,* and *Revelation*. Worship is a vital aspect of the prophetic ministry. Worship is *so important* that a church's level of revelation hinges on its level of worship.

**"'But now bring me a musician.' And it came about while the musician played, that the hand (power) of the Lord came upon Elisha." 2 Kings 3:15 (AMP)**

Worship has the ability to loosen the grip of the enemy, silence fear and doubt in the believer, and shift the atmosphere. I believe that it is one of the essential tools that will assist the Body of Christ in resolving and discontinuing these pockets of prophetic gaps throughout the churches.

> *Worship releases a distinct sound that gets the attention of heaven, and when this happens... God speaks.*

I have been to churches where the people were praising God… but He wasn't there to begin with. It was more of a theatrical display than an act of spiritual worship. When you release a real sound of worship, it releases *authority*, and *authority* announces *identity*, and *identity* establishes *dominion*. We can never underestimate the power of sincere, heartfelt corporate worship.

I strongly believe in the power of worship. People often fail to see the power because of a lack of passion and understanding in this area. They don't realize that worship is the *front door* to the presence of God... and there is no back door!

*"Passion is the vehicle that ushers you past your present state and into the presence of the Lord, where you reach the Father... and He assures you of imminent victory."*

**Passion** is simply defined as "an intense emotion." Passion is that which drives you when you can't see the way. It is the fire that purifies and validates your love and affection towards a person or a thing. Passion is what keeps you moving when others give up and throw in the towel. From personal experience, I have discovered that in life, most people who say they are "passionate" about something really aren't. Dr. Miles Monroe said, **"The proof of passion is in the pursuit."** What are you most passionate about in life? Is it family, friends, your job, your business, and other material things? Whatever you think about the most reveals the real *you*. When it comes to our Creator, our Lord, Abba, God, the King of Kings, and the Lord of Lords, it goes without saying that we ought to take full advantage of the moments when we are given the opportunity to praise and worship Him! You can never duplicate a moment in the raw presence of God. Don't miss your moment in worship! My advice to you would be to *engage* so that you can *elevate* in God. That moment may bring the prophetic word that will change your status in life forever.

> *"Never let a single moment in time affect who you are as a worshipper."* ~Tom Bynum

I can recall on several occasions when it came time to praise and worship God—I just didn't know what to expect. I was inexperienced in this area, and the whole concept of praise and worship was foreign to me. But there was always something down inside of me longing for more; the more of God that I experienced when I gave my life to Him.

I'm quite sure that if you're reading this now you can identify and relate to this to some extent, whether you have been in a dry, dead church, or in a place of spiritual drought. Perhaps the church you attend has no revelation of praise and worship. I just want to declare to you the moisture of Heaven, the oil of His glory.

> *God has always been omnipresent; we have just shut the door and stopped letting Him in!*

Here's a flashback moment for you. I remember sitting in what we used to call a "testimony service." (How many of you remember those?) For those of you who may not be familiar with the concept, a testimony service happens when an individual leads a song service and calls on people to share their praise report on how good the Lord has been. It was something we did every Sunday morning right after prayer, and right before the choir would come up and sing. Sometimes, people would take this as an opportunity to preach as well, if they had a little sermon in their spirit. I can remember it like it was yesterday; the times I had participating in the choirs and musicals. Now don't get me wrong—back then, that was as close as I got to "praise and worship!" There were times I'd be sitting in service and I'd hear music in my head, and it wasn't your typical "A and B" selections.

God *so* desires to be intimate with us. Understand this, Child of God! It is more than just God coming to you— *you've got know how to come to Him!*

Now let's look at this word "pursuit." **Pursuit** means "The act of pursuing, chasing or striving after." In other words, pushing forward, and pressing through offense, oppression, attack, distractions, disappointments, defeat, and fear. The enemy would *love* for you to become disoriented and confused when it comes to praise and worship; however, *this is where you must persevere!* Begin eliminating things and people that may try to distract you and prevent you from getting to God. You must be determined, and have a mind and heart fixed on Him. In other words... have your face set like a flint!

**"Because the Sovereign Lord helps me, I will not be disgraced. Therefore, have I set my face like flint, and I know I will not be put to shame." Isaiah 50:7 (NIV)**

I believe that the height of praise and worship is often the time when God's voice is the loudest and the clearest. There is one man in particular in the Bible who was no stranger to the posture, position, and place of worship. It was King David.

**"But now thy kingdom shall not continue: the Lord hath sought him a man after his own heart, and the Lord commanded him to be captain over his people, because thou hast not kept that which the Lord commanded thee." 1 Samuel 13:14 (KJV)**

When you hear the name *David* in relation to the Bible, one of the first things that comes to mind is that he was a worshipper. It was no secret that David found the secret to victory in the presence of the Lord. He was a man who loved God from his heart and not just his mouth! He was the eighth son of Jesse, a sheep herder, and was considered small in stature (meaning that he was short). David was not a ***perfect*** man, but he was a man ***always in pursuit of God***. David was not embarrassed or ashamed of his God. I really believe that if our men would grab hold of this revelation, many of us would be more balanced in life. David was also one of the most passionate men who ever lived.

Worship ignites the flames of the prophetic, which also produces His glory. Then the runway for spontaneous or prophetic songs is released in the place. The enemy knows this, and he will try at every turn to prevent you from touching Heaven, because *deliverance happens in the room when we touch Heaven. Breakthroughs manifest in the room when we touch Heaven. Signs, miracles, and wonders occur in the room when we touch Heaven, and the song of the Lord is released, and lives are impacted as we touch Heaven with our worship!* **You simply cannot talk about the prophetic and exclude worship**! It has been designed by God for us to reach Him, and He in turn responds back to us and ministers to us through His prophets. Worship has to be more than just a genre; it has to be a gene. If we are ever going to see Heaven rain down on us, we have to send our very best up to the Father. I speak from experience here. When I'm in an atmosphere of worship, it stirs up the prophetic anointing on my life. I can literally *feel* myself shifting to a realm in the Spirit when real worship arises. It begins to release a realm of glory that revelation resides in. God longs for us to draw near to Him and when this happens, He gives us the very best through His prophetic mouthpieces. Perhaps one of the reasons we often have such a gap in the prophetic is because we don't spend enough time in His presence. You cannot be in His Word and His presence, and not have Him put a greater hunger in you for the things of the Spirit.

**"Draw nigh to God, and he will draw nigh to you. Cleanse your hands, ye sinners; and purify your hearts, ye double minded." James 4:8 (KJV)**

**"You will show me the path of life; In Your presence is fullness of joy; In Your right hand, there are pleasures forevermore." Psalms 16:11 (AMP)**

Worship has such a major part to play in releasing the prophetic anointing. Those of you who are Apostolic and already flow in the prophetic can relate to what I'm saying. I have traveled the country, as well as outside of the USA. I have witnessed prophetic droughts in certain areas, prophetic famine, lack of prophetic activations, and even lack of prophetic training. I have been to places where people were so hungry for the prophetic, and also in places where people couldn't care less.

I specifically remember going to Sofia, Bulgaria. It was an amazing time in the Word. There was training, and impartation, and relationships being developed, perhaps for a lifetime. I had the honor of preaching at one of the biggest (if not *the* biggest) Pentecostal churches in that region. I had a translator—if you have ever preached with a translator before, you know exactly where I'm going with this. I remember that the anointing was so heavy, and the Word was just flowing. I had to remember that I had a translator assisting me so that the people could receive and be blessed, because when the anointing is flowing, you don't want to stop. You want to continue to move because of the momentum.

I have been to several cities, but a couple of them really stand out to me. One of them was Mansfield, OH. I was there with my amazing big-sister-in-the-Lord, Overseer Renea Collins. There was such a movement of God in that city, and such a need for a prophetic wind to blow through it! There were supernatural miracles that occurred, and the gifts were flowing mightily.

Another time I was in Saginaw, MI with our big brother, Bishop Alvernis and his lovely wife, Pastor Shantell Johnson. The power of worship and the prophetic was so heavy that night, with strong words of knowledge and the presence of God so thick, that you could cut it with a knife. Of course, there are many other examples, but I can't name them all. For those of you who travel and minister to the people of God, you too will be able to think of places you have visited that stand out in your mind because the people were hungry and ready! I don't know any preacher that does not want to preach in a crowd that's on fire, hungry, expectant, and waiting in faith.

As a prophet of God, one of the things that also amazes me is when I research church history. I love to read about it and watch video archives of some of the "generals" who have impacted the Body of Christ.

- **William J. Seymour:** at the forefront of the Azusa Movement
- **Charles F. Parham:** one of the men who was instrumental in spreading the Pentecostal movement
- **Maria Buelah Woodworth-Etter:** an American healing evangelist
- **John Alexander Dowie:** founder of the city of Zion, IL
- **Kathryn Kuhlman:** a graceful preacher and healing evangelist in a time when it wasn't popular for women to preach
- **A. A. Allen:** a strong healing evangelist and deliverance ministry preacher
- **Kenneth E. Hagin:** a man with a strong gift of faith
- **Dr. Oral Roberts:** ordained in both the Pentecostal Holiness Church and the United Methodist Church. Founded Oral Roberts University; moved in many miracles, signs, and wonders during his lifetime
- **Smith Wigglesworth:** a British evangelist who has been called the "Apostle of Faith"

All of these great men and women of God had something in common—they had a relentless desire to see people set free, delivered, and made whole. They were all, at some point in their lives, driven by a passion to see the gaps in the spirit-filled. God bless all of these great generals from whom we have much to learn!

There is such a great wealth of information, impartation, and influence existing in the earthly realm. Many have left their mantles and anointing for others to pick up the torch and carry it on. When we think about it, we have even lost many great generals these last couple of years. It is my heart's desire and prayer that those people walking around with a sense of entitlement, as if they are owed something, will realize that a person can't just be anointed. There's a season you go through… a process… and *then* you become anointed. I strongly believe that we are in such an hour when there will be many stirrings in the Spirit of God.

Despite the prophetic gaps that are present in certain cities and regions, the adversary has made, and will continue to make, attempts to block the flow of the gifts of the Spirit. But I declare that we are going to see also in this hour a stirring of the "Gads."

**"David left Gath and escaped to the cave of Adullam. When his brothers and his father's household heard about it, they went down to him there. All those who were in distress or in debt or discontented gathered around him, and he became their commander. About four hundred men were with him. From there David went to Mizpah in Moab and said to the king of Moab, 'Would you let my father and mother come and stay with you until I learn what God will do for me?' So, he left them with the king of Moab, and they stayed with him as long as David was in the stronghold. But the prophet Gad said to David, 'Do not stay in the strong-**

**hold. Go into the land of Judah.' So, David left and went to the forest of Hereth." 1 Samuel 22:1-5 (NIV)**

There are so many prophetic assignments in Lo-Debar in fear, in torment, and stagnating because of religion and other principalities. Fortunately, we are right on the verge of a major prophetic splurge. There are prophetic sons and daughters who are genuine, and on fire for God. We are about to see them come up from out of that hold, like in the days of King David when he and his men were all hiding in the cave. Some of you right now while reading this book may be (or know someone who is) in "the cave." The cave of *comfort*... the cave of *conforming*... the cave of *criticism*... the cave of *captivity*... the cave of a *lack of confidence*... the cave of *confusion*. I prophesy that whatever has been holding you down or back is about to snap and break off your life! You are about to prophesy like you never have before, and the wells will begin to flow from inside you. I declare that the hold is over! You've got this now!

*"Effort is the engine that will cause you to excel in your assignment and protect you from extermination."*

*Chapter 4*

# MISSING IT

*"Prophets that operate in the spirit of truth have the agenda of Heaven and not that of earth."*

*"Being a prophet of God is not a **career**, it is a **calling**. You can quit a career... but you can't quit a calling."*

**"The beginning of wisdom is this: Get wisdom. Though it cost all you have, get understanding." Proverbs 4:7 (NIV)**

**"If I have the gift of prophecy and can fathom all mysteries and all knowledge, and if I have a faith that can move mountains, but do not have love, I am nothing." 1 Corinthians 13:2 (NIV)**

Many who are now growing in prophetic revelation have genuine visions or dreams, but then arrive at a faulty interpretation because of the lack of a good foundation in the Word, and a lack of training.

You cannot draw a conclusion on anything (or any*one*, for that matter) without the basic facts. So it is with the prophetic ministry. There are some essentials to operating in the prophetic. I believe it's important to have a lifestyle of prayer, fasting, worship, and studying the Word. These are all (I believe) mandatory. Also, always keep yourself humble, so that you can remain grounded.

*"The prophetic is not based upon your internal opinions; it's based on an **eternal God,** and His Word that operates through you."*

Now sometimes, when prophets and prophetic presbytery shut the door to humility, they can miss it; and when this happens, pride enters in.

**"Pride goes before destruction, a haughty spirit before a fall." Proverbs 16:18 (NIV)**

We have to be very careful (especially as prophets) not to get the "big head!" When there's revelation that we're getting, let's always remember to measure it by the Word, and not by our own intellect. We must not allow this pattern to develop! Your prophetic gift is *not all about you*; it is there to edify, exhort, and comfort the Body of Christ.

Now, let me touch on two important areas of the teaching and preaching ministry components.

- **Exegesis:** "To lead out of." This is the exposition, extraction and explanation of a text. It is concerned with discovering the true meaning of the text, respecting its grammar, syntax and setting.

- **Eisegesis:** The reading of one's own ideas into Scripture. It means "to lead into." It is focused on making a point, perhaps even at the expense of the meaning of words.

We must be very cautious that we do not approach Scriptures from a point of Eisegesis. When this happens, the door to erroneous doctrine can be opened.

The Word is where we should always start and end. Perhaps as prophets and prophetic gifts, we should approach the prophetic more from the perspective of exegesis ("to lead out of.") In other words, standing on the Word or building on the Word will take us farther than having an assumption of what a text means. Nobody in their right mind will go out on the water unless they know they have the adequate support that they need to hold them above water. When we have the Word with the prophetic, it will keep us above the water!

When we minister the Word of the Lord, it must be "God-breathed," not "man-manufactured." Man can manufacture appliances, cars, homes, and electronics, but man cannot manufacture the anointing of the Holy Spirit. As a prophet or prophetic presbytery, I must be in a position where I am standing on something. That something I'm referring to is the Word. Before you were ever a prophet with a ministry gift, God *was* and *is* and *will always be*. He is the beginning and the end.

**"In the beginning God (Elohim) created [by forming from [nothing] the heavens and the earth. The earth was formless and void or a waste and emptiness, and darkness was upon the face of the deep [primeval ocean that covered the unformed earth]. The Spirit of God was moving (hovering, brooding) over the face of the waters." Genesis 1:1-3 (AMP)**

**"In the beginning [before all time] was the Word (Christ), and the Word was with God, and the Word was God Himself. He was [continually existing] in the beginning [co-eternally] with God. All things were made and came into existence through Him; and without Him not even one thing was made that has come into being." John 1:1-3 (AMP)**

We cannot be the prophetic gift that we have been called to be without the foundation of the Word. Here are a few more references:

**"The Spirit of the Lord spake by me, and his word was in my tongue." 2 Samuel 23:2 (KJV)**

"Your word is a lamp to my feet and a light to my path." Psalms 119:105 (AMP)

"Jesus answered, 'It is written: "Man shall not live on bread alone, but on every word that comes from the mouth of God."'" Matthew 4:4 (NIV)

"Then said Jesus to those Jews which believed on him, if ye continue in my word, then are ye my disciples indeed." John 8:31 (KJV)

"If ye abide in me, and my words abide in you, ye shall ask what ye will, and it shall be done unto you." John 15:7 (KJV)

"And now, brethren, I commend you to God, and to the word of his grace, which is able to build you up, and to give you an inheritance among all them which are sanctified." Acts 20:32 (KJV)

"For the word of God is alive and active. Sharper than any double-edged sword, it penetrates even to dividing soul and spirit, joints and marrow; it judges the thoughts and attitudes of the heart." Hebrews 4:12 (NIV)

"Wherefore lay apart all filthiness and superfluity of naughtiness, and receive with meekness the engrafted word, which is able to save your souls." James 1:21 (KJV)

"Being born again, not of corruptible seed, but of incorruptible, by the word of God, which liveth and abideth forever." 1 Peter 1:23 (KJV)

"Study to shew thyself approved unto God, a workman that needeth not to be ashamed, rightly dividing the word of truth." 2 Timothy 2:15 (KJV)

**"Let the message of Christ dwell among you richly as you teach and admonish one another with all wisdom through psalms, hymns, and songs from the Spirit, singing to God with gratitude in your hearts." Colossians 3:16 (NIV)**

Some of the people who are claiming to be prophetic are coming up with some "off-the-wall" stuff these days! But let's learn to keep these two things in the right places. I just noticed that a lot of prophetic people are so "out there" that it's weird. Now, I'm not knocking coming out of the box; however, keeping balance and order to the prophetic ministry is essential.

*"Before you enter into the major league of the prophetic, it is important that you go through the minors."*

God spoke to my heart several months ago, and He stated that there is about to be released in this new season a dimension of miracles in the prophetic ministry like we've never seen before. The prophets of God will move in the supernatural on a regular basis, and signs and wonders will become the norm, with an unbelievably fresh fire.

**"Trust in the Lord with all your heart and lean not on your own understanding; in all your ways submit to him, and he will make your paths straight." Proverbs 3:5-6 (NIV)**

### Women in Prophetic Ministry

One of the things that I have noticed over the years is a misunderstanding of Scripture when it comes to what place women have in prophetic ministry (or just in ministry, period).

I know that there are a lot of opinions on the subject and I don't want to go too deeply into this, because I know that my wife is called of God, and perhaps someday, even into the office of an apostle. The reality is that things along this line can't be ignored any longer. The fact is that I know many women who are much anointed and have a genuine call of God on their lives, and I'll go on record and say that many of these women have the hand of God on them. They are doing a better job than some of the men who confess that they have the call of God on their lives (no disrespect meant to the men who really do have a genuine call on their lives.)

My question is, "Who in the world has made man a God?" The One who is the author and finisher! He is the One who appoints and anoints His vessels for service. If we are not careful as believers, we can let our opinions build a wall that will prevent us from walking into everything that the Lord has for us. Even in the Bible, we can see that the spirit of prophecy was not just restricted to men. We know from Genesis that God has called men to be the head.

**"To the woman he said, "I will make your pains in child bearing very severe; with painful labor you will give birth to children. Your desire will be for your husband, and he will rule over you." Genesis 3:16 (NIV)**

The Book of **Ephesians** tells us:

**"Submit to one another out of reverence for Christ. Wives, submit yourselves to your own husbands, as you do to the Lord. For the husband is the head of the wife as Christ is the head of the church, his body, of which he is the Savior." Ephesians 5:21-23 (NIV)**

Of course, there are several other references to men being the head of the household, but the focus here is not so much the household, but rather the ministry. I grew up in an area where there wasn't much acknowledgement of women in a certain level of ministry, but I am amazed to see how the glass ceiling has shattered for many women in the church. I've said it before and I'll say it again: *God is not building a church based on religion, but on relationship.* The truth is that often, churches don't have an issue with a *form* of the church; the problem lies with *becoming* the church!

The Bible mentions at least ten women who were used in the prophetic ministry, or in the office of a prophet—five each in the Old and New Testaments (the number five represents the number of grace). I believe that this is very much a prophetic representation of the spirit of prophecy among the women of God in the Scriptures. I believe that women in ministry are just as important as men are. We need them both. Our focus and objective should always be on unification, not division. Operating in the prophetic has nothing to do with your gender—it has everything to do with God, and whoever is available to be a conduit for His glory. The Spirit of the Lord is nowhere in this foolishness. Let the women of God who are thoroughbreds arise, soar, conquer, and prophesy!

**Old Testament References:**

- **Miriam: Exodus 15:20-21 (NIV)**
  **"Then Miriam the prophet, Aaron's sister, took a timbrel in her hand, and all the women followed her, with timbrels and dancing. Miriam sang to them:**

  > **'Sing to the Lord,**
  > **for he is highly exalted.**
  > **Both horse and driver**
  > **he has hurled into the sea.'"**

- **Deborah: Judges 4:4 (NIV)**
  **"Now Deborah, a prophet, the wife of Lappidoth, was leading Israel at that time. She held court under**

the Palm of Deborah between Ramah and Bethel in the hill country of Ephraim, and the Israelites went up to her to have their disputes decided."

- Huldah: 2 Kings 22:14-20 (NIV)
  "Hilkiah the priest, Ahikam, Akbor, Shaphan and Asaiah went to speak to the prophet Huldah, who was the wife of Shallum son of Tikvah, the son of Harhas, keeper of the wardrobe. She lived in Jerusalem, in the New Quarter. She said to them, "This is what the Lord, the God of Israel, says: Tell the man who sent you to me, 'This is what the Lord says: I am going to bring disaster on this place and its people, according to everything written in the book the king of Judah has read. Because they have forsaken me and burned incense to other gods and aroused my anger by all the idols their hands have made, my anger will burn against this place and will not be quenched.' Tell the king of Judah, who sent you to inquire of the Lord, 'This is what the Lord, the God of Israel, says concerning the words that you heard: Because your heart was responsive and you humbled yourself before the Lord when you heard what I have spoken against this place and its people—that they would become a curse and be laid waste—and because you tore your robes and wept in my presence, I also have heard you, declares the Lord. Therefore, I will gather you to your ancestors, and you will be buried in peace. Your eyes will not see all the disaster I am going to bring on this place." So they took her answer back to the king."

- Noadiah: Nehemiah 6:14 (NIV)
  "Remember Tobiah and Sanballat, my God, because of what they have done; remember also the prophet Noadiah and how she and the rest of the prophets have been trying to intimidate me. So the

wall was completed on the twenty-fifth of Elul, in fifty-two days."

- The Prophet Isaiah's wife: Isaiah 8:3 (NIV)
"The Lord said to me, 'Take a large scroll and write on it with an ordinary pen: Maher-Shalal-Hash-Baz.' So, I called in Uriah the priest and Zechariah son of Jeberekiah as reliable witnesses for me. Then I made love to the prophetess, and she conceived and gave birth to a son. And the Lord said to me, 'Name him Maher-Shalal-Hash-Baz.'"

**New Testament References:**

- Anna: Luke 2:36-38 (NIV)
"There was also a prophet, Anna, the daughter of Penuel, of the tribe of Asher. She was very old; she had lived with her husband seven years after her marriage, and then was a widow until she was eighty-four. She never left the temple but worshiped night and day, fasting and praying. Coming up to them at that very moment, she gave thanks to God and spoke about the child to all who were looking forward to the redemption of Jerusalem."

- The four daughters of Philip the evangelist: Acts 21:8-9 (NIV)
"We continued our voyage from Tyre and landed at Ptolemais, where we greeted the brothers and sisters and stayed with them for a day. Leaving the next day, we reached Caesarea and stayed at the house of Philip, the evangelist, one of the Seven. He had four unmarried daughters who prophesied."

"But mark this: There will be terrible times in the last days. People will be lovers of themselves, lovers of money, boastful, proud, abusive, disobedient to their parents, ungrateful, unholy, without love, unforgiving, slanderous, without self-control, brutal, not lovers of the good, treacherous, rash, conceited, lovers of pleasure rather than lovers of God—having a form of godliness but denying its power. Have nothing to do with such people." 2 Timothy 3:1-5 (NIV)

Isn't it ironic how Timothy says, "Have nothing to do with such people?" You don't need anyone in your life to be a Jesse and try to block the lane to your prophetic destiny. David had the call, but his father Jesse almost messed it up. He was thinking "in the flesh," and not being spiritual. He attempted to bring everyone else before the Prophet Samuel but David! Let's look at this story found in **1 Samuel**.

"The Lord said to Samuel, 'How long will you mourn for Saul, since I have rejected him as king over Israel? Fill your horn with oil and be on your way; I am sending you to Jesse of Bethlehem. I have chosen one of his sons to be king.' But Samuel said, 'How can I go? If Saul hears about it, he will kill me.' The Lord said, 'Take a heifer with you and say, "I have come to sacrifice to the Lord." Invite Jesse to the sacrifice, and I will show you what to do. You are to anoint for me the one I indicate.' Samuel did what the Lord said. When he arrived at Bethlehem, the elders of the town trembled when they met him. They asked, 'Do you come in peace?' Samuel replied, 'Yes, in peace; I have come to sacrifice to the Lord. Consecrate yourselves and come to the sacrifice with me.' Then he consecrated Jesse and his sons and invited them to the sacrifice.

When they arrived, Samuel saw Eliab and thought, 'Surely the Lord's anointed stands here before the Lord.' But the Lord said to Samuel, 'Do not consider his appearance or his height, for I have rejected him. The Lord does not look at the things people look at. People look at the outward appearance, but the Lord looks at the heart.' Then Jesse called Abinadab and had him pass in front of Samuel. But Samuel said, 'The Lord has not chosen this one either.' Jesse then had Shammah pass by, but Samuel said, 'Nor has the Lord chosen this one.' Jesse had seven of his sons pass before Samuel, but Samuel said to him, 'The Lord has not chosen these.' So he asked Jesse, 'Are these all the sons you have?'

'There is still the youngest,' Jesse answered. 'He is tending the sheep.' Samuel said, 'Send for him; we will not sit down until he arrives.' So he sent for him and had him brought in. He was glowing with health and had a fine appearance and handsome features. Then the Lord said, 'Rise and anoint him; this is the one.' So Samuel took the horn of oil and anointed him in the presence of his brothers, and from that day on the Spirit of the Lord came powerfully upon David. Samuel then went to Ramah." 1 Samuel 16:1-13 (NIV)

There will be people that come into your life either to *inspire you* or *expire you*. You have been "chosen to be overlooked but noticed to be next." Some things in reference to your assignment have been chosen by God for you to encounter—for instance, being disregarded and overlooked. Often, God has to hide you so that others won't see you, and so that He can ultimately receive the glory as you are elevated. You won't be tainted or stained by inappropriate things that are not related to your purpose, so that when it's your time, you cannot and will not be denied! In your lifetime, you will probably even encounter "Jesse".

These are people who can't see that God's hand is on your life. They think it should be them and not you, or that you're too young to be a prophet or a leader—you don't even have degrees or certificates! There are so many reasons why people will try to stand in your way, but I believe that all of you reading this right now get exactly what I'm saying. Jesse went down the line, naming all of his sons, and didn't even think to consider David until last. I just want to declare to anyone who may be experiencing anything like this, that God is about to clear the lane for you to have access and to score. In the words of Bishop T. D. Jakes, "Get ready, get ready, get ready!"

## Chapter 5

# SENSITIVITY

*"When it comes to the prophetic, there's either sensitivity or stupidity, and no room for self."*

*"The result of the right impartation is establishment."*
~Apostle John Eckhardt, "God Still Speaks"

**"And we have the prophetic word [made] firmer still. You will do well to pay close attention to it as to a lamp shining in a dismal (squalid and dark) place, until the day breaks through [the gloom] and the Morning Star rises (comes into being) in your hearts. [Yet] first [you must] understand this, that no prophecy of Scripture is [a matter] of any personal or private or special interpretation (loosening, solving). For no prophecy ever originated because some man willed it [to do so–it never came by human impulse], but men spoke from God who were borne along (moved and impelled) by the Holy Spirit." 2 Peter 1:19-21 (AMP)**

I remember being a young minister in my late teens, when I didn't really know and understand the voice of the Lord as I do today. I believe that there was always something deep in me that wanted more of Him, even in those early days. Because of my upbringing and environment, certain core beliefs had developed, and many of them were actually blocking me from hearing the voice of the Lord in that season of my life.

I grew up in the Pentecostal Assemblies of the World, and back then, we didn't have prophetic ministry or prophetic worship in most of our churches. It was just "church as usual." But as time passed, I noticed that something was shifting in my spirit. I began to hear things and see things, and I didn't quite understand what was going on.

I will never forget when God began to deal with me in such a strong way. Long story short, I found myself visiting this church that I had seen on television. During one of the mid-week services, I was called out, and the man of God at that time began to call me out and minister prophetically over my life. My first reaction was to be defensive, but I heard the voice of the Lord saying, "This is *me*, John! Open up and just give it all to me." I remember saying, "Yes, God!" Eventually, I began this prophetic journey that would change the direction of my life forever.

**"Do not neglect your gift, which was given you through prophecy, when the body of elders laid their hands on you." 1 Timothy 4:14 (NIV)**

My prophetic calling began to grow, and my spiritual appetite began to change. I was literally going through "religious detox."

My desire for the Word of the Lord changed, and my desire for His presence grew stronger. I began my season of learning about sensitivity to the things of the Spirit of God. (I must admit—it has been a journey worth the discovery.) I have lost friends and family members in the process, and although I didn't get it then, I now know without a doubt that it was for my good. Some of my friends at the time thought that it was kind of odd that I had such a heart for worship, prayer, and the things of God. I can remember, even as a teenager, being in church on a Saturday in prayer every weekend without fail. I was in church every Sunday morning for Sunday school, prayer, and the worship service, then back for the afternoon service. Then I would connect with some of my friends who loved church and we would visit what is now Bishop Willie James Campbell's church. This had become the norm for me as a young man. I have learned quite a bit and will never take for granted what I got sitting under the church mothers on Sunday, while the other kids would go outside and play. I guess even before I knew the Lord, I was destined to stand out.

When I was in high school, I was so into "church" that I almost missed my high school prom. I didn't realize how really "religious" I was. Not that I didn't have any prospects, but I just really did not have any desire to hang in that crowd. At the last minute, I called one of my boys and he called another and we all went stag to our prom. No girls—just a few of us guys. These were some of my best friends in high school. I could go on and on, but I'll spare you the details. I thought in my mind that I really *knew* God, but I discovered that this wasn't the case. I had the "appearance" of a church goer, but I wasn't walking in my destiny back then. It wasn't until my relationships began to change and I began to step out of the box I had allowed the spirit of religion to build in me that I really began to embrace my destiny.

> *We can sit around all day and blame others for what's going on in our lives, but at the end of the day, we have to admit that we have played a part in what has happened to us.*

You may be reading this right now, and thinking back, there was a time in your life where you had to make a tough decision. It's like that commercial on TV... "Should I stay or should I go?" Some of us find ourselves stuck in a "religious" church setting, and whenever the Spirit of God desires to move, the church shuts it down. Many people are crying all over the Body of Christ. They are hungry for truth, and for the rawness of the Spirit of God. My heart goes out to the many who are gifted with good intentions, and who are faithful and love their churches. They are trapped in controlling places where they are dealing with a strong spirit of religion, but there's no prophetic in sight, limited revelation, no warfare praying, and of course, no prophetic worship. The Apostle Paul even discussed this in the New Testament.

**"Do not quench [subdue, or be unresponsive to the working and guidance of] the [Holy] Spirit. Do not scorn or reject gifts of prophecy or prophecies [spoken revelations—words of instruction or exhortation or warning]." 1 Thessalonians 5:19-20 (AMP)**

I want to help you answer this question. It's time to go! I am learning more and more each day that things don't just happen! You are like the artist with the paintbrush in his hand; you can either paint a masterpiece or just "conform." I want to bring your attention to this "spirit of religion." It is literally a spirit that is committed to convenience. It is a spirit that can dull or destroy spiritual sensitivity if you give it the power to do so. It will spread like a cancer in your spirit, and it's designed to desensitize you from the gifts of the Spirit. As a Holy Ghost-filled believer and born-again Christian, you have the power to decree, declare, and prophesy.

Let's take it a step further. Manifestation and activity of religious spirits require a friendly union between the "flesh" (the fallen human nature) and demons. It is not solely demonic activity, so being around them requires a different spiritual response.

Jesus had no trouble with demons—the Scriptures tell us that "the demons bowed and fled." The Pharisees were a different matter. Religious spirits did not bow down and obey them, because of the free will element that was involved.

To interact with them is like dealing with a hybrid of demon and human. The human component makes it difficult to remove the demonic, because the human part is enjoying the fellowship and power the demon gives it, and does not want it to leave. Deliverance will not happen without the humans' will agreeing to it.

How to recognize them:

- Religious spirits **oppress and persecute others**, usually true believers. They do this in the name of God.
- They **criticize others almost constantly**, and recruit others to join them.
- They are **controlling and legalistic**, and rigid in their opinions.
- They are very **unforgiving** of the wrong they accuse you of doing.
- Their **religious zeal, spirituality, and righteousness are not of God**.
- They have **no personal relationship with God**, just a religious agenda that they want followed, with them in control.
- The **focus is on perfection**, not progress.
- They are often **proud and arrogant**.
- They **find fault with others** but not with themselves.
- They **know how to tear down**, but not to build up.
- They are often **unable to receive correction and instruction**.
- They **will not listen to man**, only to God.
- They **will not submit to human authority**, unless that authority exalts them.
- They **believe that God has appointed them to fix you**, and that God cannot do it without them.
- **They are self-appointed to fix everything wrong in *your* life**, but they "fix" you by tearing you down, destroying you, and criticizing everything they think is wrong with you.

- Religious spirits are **suspicious of every move of God as being from the devil**. They watch and study and do not believe it. It spreads the dispositions of doubt. They say that if God did not do it before, then He cannot be doing it now.
- **God is not allowed to do anything they do not understand**. They forget that the devil copies God. God does not copy the devil.
- They **glory in yesterday, but not today**, unless they are in the center of it.
- They **will not join in any group outside of their own** and **will forbid you to do the same**. "We have all the truth." *Cult thinking*.
- **They do not allow you to go anywhere else except their church,** or you will be defiled.
- They **do not understand the work of grace** in someone's life.
- They take a **false stand on dreams and visions**. They say that theirs are okay, but not yours.
- **There's no room for God to work in their life**. They think that they are already perfect.
- They may have started out as Spirit-filled, but they **think they can perfect themselves in the flesh**.
- They will **put religious curses on innocent people**.
- **If unchecked, they will progress to the demonic**, and then will need deliverance.
- They **make false accusations, then justify with irrelevant Scripture, to "sanctify" the evil that is spoken.** *This can be the most twisted and confusing experience.*

I felt as though I needed to share this. This is prevalent in many of our churches. The prophetic axes in the church has become dull or desensitized because of this spirit. *But I declare that we are going to see a prophetic release so strong, that the religious spirit that has opposed it for years will begin to lose its grip, and lives will be free,* **because where the Spirit of the Lord is, there is freedom**!

"Now the Lord is the Spirit, and where the Spirit of the Lord is, there is liberty [emancipation from bondage, true freedom]." 2 Corinthian 3:17 (AMP)

"Blessed are they which do hunger and thirst after righteousness: for they shall be filled." Matthew 5:6 (KJV)

You have to be *hungry* for the things of the Spirit. When this begins to happen, you spark the flame of sensitivity. Things will start changing as you submit to the change. Think about it! Life is designed with twists and turns, ups and downs, and misunderstandings, but it's important that we learn from them! Life is full of the unexpected, but we must continue to pursue after the heart of God, just as King David did.

*I declare that there will be an emergence of the Davids, and of people who will long for the raw presence of God. The restructuring and rebuilding of the tabernacles of David, a release of the Key of David in the earth that will turn and shift this generation to the heart of the Father.*

I declare a "new breed." A kingdom-minded culture that will shake the foundations of the spirit of religion, and the presence of God will move in such a way that many would come to know Him who knew not religion, for *"Many have known Me through religion,"* saith the Lord, *"but the generation of now will know Me by relationship, for they have not been tainted by doctrines and sayings of men, for where I shift they will shift, what I release they shall release in the earth with a passion for Me,"* saith the Lord.

"I see the young lions are stirring in the spirit, for the time of the great awakening is upon us, the lions are coming to the church," saith the Lord, *"the lions are coming, this sound will be heard near and far, for others will hear a distinct sound and come out of hiding, for many have been waiting for the roar of thunder, the sound of worship to shake the heavens and release sons and daughters in the earth. So, get ready,"* saith the Lord, *"the great awakening in upon us... this generation, they will reveal My glory in such a way,"* saith the Lord. I sense a momentum shift! (*Prophecy*)

Sensitivity to the things of the Lord doesn't just happen overnight. It has to be developed over a period of time. Every ministry gift has a learning season, whether you are an apostle, prophet, pastor, teacher or evangelist.

To really be able to operate in the office of the prophet, the unction alone will not be acceptable. You're going to need more than **Unction**; you're going to need **Understanding**. Your flesh will have to **Undergo** a crucifixion, you'll have to live a life as a servant of God **Unashamed**, you'll have to **Unattach** yourself from people's opinion of you. You'll have to become **Unrelenting** for His presence and Word, because if by chance you don't, you will become **Unskilled** and never be able to **Unleash** all of what God has on the inside of you!

> *"The prophetic involves having His mind and His heart and losing yours. This is one sure way that the channel of the prophetic will open wide unto you."*

One major thing when it comes to sensitivity is the capacity to hear and distinguish the difference between *God's voice* and *your voice*. When you are watching TV, each channel falls into a specific category. You have the shopping channels, the news channels, the National Geographic channel, movie channels, comedy channels, kids programming channels, and of course, the most important ones—the cooking channels! When it comes to the spiritual gifting, however, there is one specific channel, and we who are prophetic need to tune in to that one.

I remember as a kid, when I was listening to my favorite radio station, and my favorite song would come on. I would move the radio into another room in the apartment, and all of sudden, the clear signal that I had when it was in the other room was gone, and I would be hearing two different stations.

Oftentimes as believers, we struggle with hearing the voice of God and that which is relative to the prophetic. It becomes discouraging, distracting, and disappointing when you can't hear what you need to hear. God wants to commune with you as His child, daily. He wants to have an ongoing and open relationship with you. It's important to consider your current position. It has been said that "the higher the antenna extends in the air, the stronger the signal." We must learn how to adjust to a certain "position" in God, so that we can begin to hear His voice regularly.

One of the secrets that I have discovered to knowing and recognizing the voice of God is just being alone with Him! We must learn how to get away sometimes and have one-on-one time with the Lord. The beginning of learning to hear the voice of God starts by having faith in His Word.

You must mature in your hearing so that you are not stuck on what God said in the past but are able to hear what He is saying right now. Some people stay trapped in an 8-track tape mentality, when what they really need is HiDef!

**"But he answered and said, 'It is written, Man shall not live by bread alone, but by every word that proceedeth out of the mouth of God.'" Matthew 4:4 (KJV)**

You must learn the art of being alone with Him in private before you can be public with Him. It's alright to spend time with the Father first to get to know His mind and heart.

Sometimes, people struggle to hear God, not because He isn't speaking, but often because their heart has a defect and is deficient. Check your heart regularly. Those of us who have taken a science class know that the heart is a muscle that assists in pumping blood throughout the body. The blood of course is associated with life. The Bible says, **"The life is in the blood."** (See **Leviticus 17:11**) In the life of every believer, the prophetic can become the spiritual pump that releases life in the body.

**"Create in me a clean heart, O God; and renew a right spirit within me." Psalms 51:10 (KJV)**

**"The sheep that are My own hear My voice and listen to Me; I know them, and they follow Me. And I give them eternal life, and they will never, ever [by any means] perish; and no one will ever snatch them out of My hand." John 10:27-28 (AMP)**

**"So, faith comes from hearing [what is told], and what is heard comes by the [preaching of the] message concerning Christ." Romans 10:17 (AMP)**

**"Whoever has ears, let them hear what the Spirit says to the churches. To the one who is victorious, I will give some of the hidden manna. I will also give that person a white stone with a new name written on it, known only to the one who receives it." Revelation 2:17 (NIV)**

**"Whether you turn to the right or to the left, your ears will hear a voice behind you, saying, "This is the way; walk in it." Isaiah 30:21 (NIV)**

**H.E.A.R.I.N.G.** is...

**H**umbling yourself
**E**ngaging Him and others
**A**ccessing revelations
**R**edirecting yourself
**I**ntentional about
**N**arrowing in on
**G**od

**VOICE:**

"There's **V**ictory **O**nly by His **I**nstructions, which produce **C**larity and the **E**xceptional life!"

It is very beneficial for the believer to have faith in hearing the voice of the Lord through the ministry of the prophetic.

HEARING GOD'S VOICE THROUGH THE PROPHETIC:

- **Protects** you
- **Preserves** you
- **Perfects** you
- **Positions** you
- Reveals the **Possibilities**
- Releases **Power**
- Avoids the **Premature**
- **Prepares** you
- **Propels** you
- Gives you clarity on your **Purpose**

**"But as it is written, 'Eye hath not seen, nor ear heard, neither have entered into the heart of man, the things which God hath prepared for them that love him.' But God hath revealed them unto us by his Spirit: for the Spirit searcheth all things, yea, the deep things of God. For what man knoweth the things of a man, save the**

spirit of man, which is in him? Even so the things of God knoweth no man, but the Spirit of God. Now we have received, not the spirit of the world, but the spirit which is of God; that we might know the things that are freely given to us of God. Which things also we speak, not in the words which man's wisdom teacheth, but which the Holy Ghost teacheth; comparing spiritual things with spiritual. But the natural man receiveth not the things of the Spirit of God: for they are foolishness unto him: neither can he know them, because they are spiritually discerned. But he that is spiritual judgeth all things, yet he himself is judged of no man. For who hath known the mind of the Lord, that he may instruct him? but we have the mind of Christ." 1 Corinthians 2:9-14 (KJV)

## Chapter 6

# ORGANIC VS. ARTIFICIAL PROPHETIC MINISTRY

"***Organic prophecy*** *is birthed from the **spirit** and the **artificial prophecy** is birthed from the **soul**.*"

**Organic** (according to Merriam-Webster) means "of, relating to, yielding, or involving the use of food produced with the use of feed or fertilizer of plant or animal origin without employment of chemically formulated fertilizers, growth stimulants, antibiotics, or pesticides."

**Artificial** means "lacking in natural or spontaneous quality." One of the interesting words that I have discovered that is relative to *artificial* is the word "cunning." Most of us are familiar with the terminology in reference to the fox—the animal with an innate desire to manipulate, deceive, and engineer a situation to its own advantage.

Let's look at this from another perspective. For instance, in your grocery store, there is a produce section. In the produce area, there is either regular or organic produce. When it comes to organic produce, it generally costs more, but it's much healthier for you than your traditional produce. Produce that is not organic runs the risk of being tainted, enhanced with steroids and other outside chemicals—and you guessed it! This type of produce doesn't cost as much.

Now, let's look at this from a prophetic perspective. Many people that operate in prophetic ministry have to be very aware not to allow outside influences to dictate or determine their level of flow.

There is so much going on these days in the prophetic that many ministries don't want anything to do with it. I can't begin to tell you how many pastors and leaders have been turned off when it comes to the prophetic gift. The essence and the continuity of the assignment of this gift have been influenced and contaminated by so many outside elements. The prophetic does not exist to prostitute, pimp, rape, rob or manipulate the people of God! It exists to launch others out, inspire them, encourage them, strengthen them, and assist in aligning them with their destiny.

The truth is that people want to know *who they are* and *where they belong.* The world has even leaned towards the psychic and other means to get some type of direction for their lives.

Psychics operate illegally in the spirit realm and the enemy uses this medium to detach you from the real prophets of God and the things of God. Now, on the other hand, the true prophets of God have the authority and legal access in the spirit realm and they aid in keeping you attached to the Spirit of God and the things of God.

This is why we need the original *and* the organic in the prophetic ministry—to turn our attention back to the heart of the Father. All of this black magic, tarot cards, Ouija boards, crystal balls, and all these other types of mediums really fall under an artificial category. It has never been the intention of God for His people to look to other resources and avenues for direction and confirmation.

*"A true call or confirmation of the prophet is like a sign, it doesn't point to itself, but guides and directs you to a destination."*

Remember when King Saul was in "a bit of a situation?" He needed a word from the Lord, and the heavens appeared to have been closed over him. This is something that we see too often we see in the Body of Christ. What was powerful about this time in the life of King Saul was when the spirit of the prophet Samuel appeared and prophesied over his life again. Let me just say that you cannot replace the organic prophet gift with an artificial one. Now, I have seen many who are functioning in both of these capacities.

There will never be a comparison between the two, but always a difference; just as night is the opposite of day, hot is the opposite of cold, and in the opposite of out!

*"Divination is a doorway into the spirit of error. If it knocks at your door, don't answer it."*

**"In those days, the Philistines gathered their forces to fight against Israel. Achish said to David, 'You must understand that you and your men will accompany me in the army.' David said, 'Then you will see for yourself what your servant can do.' Achish replied, 'Very well, I will make you my bodyguard for life.'"**

**Saul and the Medium at Endor**

**"Now Samuel was dead, and all Israel had mourned for him and buried him in his own town of Ramah. Saul had expelled the mediums and spiritists from the land. The Philistines assembled and came and set up camp at Shunem, while Saul gathered all Israel and set up camp at Gilboa. When Saul saw the Philistine army, he was afraid; terror filled his heart. He inquired of the Lord,**

but the Lord did not answer him by dreams or Urim or prophets. Saul then said to his attendants, 'Find me a woman who is a medium, so I may go and inquire of her.'"

"'There is one in Endor,' they said. So Saul disguised himself, putting on other clothes, and at night he and two men went to the woman. 'Consult a spirit for me,' he said, 'and bring up for me the one I name.' But the woman said to him, 'Surely you know what Saul has done. He has cut off the mediums and spiritists from the land. Why have you set a trap for my life to bring about my death?' Saul swore to her by the Lord, 'As surely as the Lord lives, you will not be punished for this.' Then the woman asked, 'Whom shall I bring up for you?' 'Bring up Samuel,' he said. When the woman saw Samuel, she cried out at the top of her voice and said to Saul, 'Why have you deceived me? You are Saul!' The king said to her, 'Don't be afraid. What do you see?' The woman said, 'I see a ghostly figure coming up out of the earth.' 'What does he look like?' he asked. 'An old man wearing a robe is coming up,' she said."

"Then Saul knew it was Samuel, and he bowed down and prostrated himself with his face to the ground. Samuel said to Saul, 'Why have you disturbed me by bringing me up?'

'I am in great distress,' Saul said. 'The Philistines are fighting against me, and God has departed from me. He no longer answers me, either by prophets or by dreams. So I have called on you to tell me what to do.' Samuel said, 'Why do you consult me, now that the Lord has departed from you and become your enemy? The Lord has done what he predicted through me. The Lord has torn the kingdom out of your hands and given it to one of your neighbors—to David. Because you did not obey the Lord or carry out his fierce wrath against the

**Amalekites, the Lord has done this to you today. The Lord will deliver both Israel and you into the hands of the Philistines, and tomorrow you and your sons will be with me. The Lord will also give the army of Israel into the hands of the Philistines.'" 1 Samuel 28:1-19 (NIV)**

As we see here in this text, it not wise to try to create something that only God can supply. Many times in life, we are searching for answers, and it can be easy to lean towards something that may grant us a "fast resolution." King Saul had been granted access to a prophet of God by the name of Samuel, in whom "none of his words ever fell to the ground." When a crisis arose, King Saul began to panic. He had already made his stance on how he felt about psychics and mediums very clear, but when the pressure was on... he sought out the *very thing* that he had forbidden in the kingdom.

Believer, even though you may think you are getting away with something, or "putting one over on God," God always has a way of revealing who He is! As prophetic people, we can all learn from this story... *if we are patient and just trust God, it will happen in His timing*. Let's not try to step into a season without first finding God's timing. I actually have a saying that goes, "The design is for the horse to pull the carriage, not the carriage to pull the horse!" *Selah*.

When I am organically prophetic, there's a sense of *authenticity*, *purity*, and *integrity*. I'm not moved by money, popularity, politics, and other enticements or incentives that may present themselves.

When I'm organically prophetic, it's because I've spent the time in the Word and in His presence. I know Him, and He knows me. I can't be Bishop Jakes, Bishop I. V. Hilliard, Apostle John Eckhardt, Juanita Bynum, Benny Hinn, Joyce Meyer, Creflo Dollar or even the likes of Brian Carn.

I have to be *me*, and that entails being *authentic*, *original*, and *organic*. I trust you get my point here!

**"For those who are led by the spirit of God are the children of God." Romans 8:14 (NIV)**

*"A true prophet is not moved by materialism but is moved by the manifestation and the leading of the Spirit of God."*

As a prophet or prophetic gift, I must learn to guard and protect my heart from things such as divination and prophetic witchcraft; those things where someone uses their "gift" to manipulate situations and people. I must learn to shield my spirit with the Word, so that these temptations that may come will be deflected. I must also take care not to be blind to the things of God, but remain a threat to the devil. If I don't position the Word in my heart and life, I subject myself to becoming an artificial prophet or ministry gift. When I'm artificial, it's often because there's been a lack of time in which I involve myself with the things of God.

*Chapter 7*

# PROPHETS AND PROFITS

*"A true prophet is attracted to the glory; false prophets are attracted to making up or manipulating a story."*

*"As a prophet never take it upon yourself to make up a prophetic word. Don't have a Moses moment and smite the prophetic rock."*

Real prophets don't *duplicate*. They *supplicate*, then *demonstrate* what God releases and designates, and then they *annihilate*.

**There is such a need for the real prophets to arise!**

True *prophets* are addicted to the Word and attracted to the presence of the Lord and to the glory that's found in worship. It's the ones who are not that we have to be concerned with. *Profits* are moved by, and attracted to, the things of the world.

Five Things to Know About the Office of the Prophet:

- There is an ongoing lifestyle of **Intimacy** with the Father
- There is an ongoing lifestyle of **Wisdom**
- There is an ongoing lifestyle of **Revelation**
- There is an ongoing lifestyle of **Prayer** and **Worship**
- There is an ongoing lifestyle of **Holiness**

What are some other functions that set the prophet apart?

One of the first goals of the prophetic ministry is to *bring the Body of Christ to a place of maturity*. The only way to know that the Body of Christ is in a place of maturity is when believers are walking in faith, love, and hope. Not *settling* but *soaring* in the things of God.

*"The prophet is to the church what the rudder is to the ship, they steer you in the direction you're supposed to go, even at those times in life when you're off course, the prophet redirects your course!"*

The second goal of the prophet is to *bring believers to a full knowledge of the Lord*. They should never become the center of the attention or focus. All roads should lead to Christ.

**"My people are destroyed from lack of knowledge. Because you have rejected knowledge, I also reject you as my priests; because you have ignored the law of your God, I also will ignore your children." Hosea 4:6 (NIV)**

The word *lack* in this text refers to "darkness," "misguided perspective" or "being trapped in a complacent place or state of being." So many people fall short, either because of what they think they know, or because of what they think they don't need. When this text says, "My people are destroyed for a lack of knowledge," this is a *direct word*. Who are "my people" that are referenced here? My apostles (those who *govern*), my prophets (those who *guide*), my pastors (those who *guard*), my evangelists (those who *gather*), my teachers (those who *ground* you), and finally, the house of God at large, from laity to leadership.

The third goal of the prophet is to help prepare believers for the ministry that God has called them into. This is one of my favorite tasks. I love seeing people walking into their prophetic destinies!

In order to be a prophet, the individual had to have a message from God in the form of special revelation, had to have guidance regarding its declaration so that it would be given forth accurately, and the message itself had to have the authority of God. The prophetic office, therefore, was different from the teaching office in that the teaching office had no more authority than the Scripture upon which it was based, whereas the prophetic office had its authority in the experience of divine reception and communication of truth. This is why there is such a great need for prophetic preaching and teaching in the Body of Christ. The written logos is great but when I'm in a situation, I don't need the Greek, Hebrew, and your interpretation of the Bible. I need a Rhema!

*"True prophetic words from the prophets of God come from the heart of heaven and not the heart of man."*

What's scary is that sometimes you can't even tell that some of these prophets and prophetic gifts have spent time with the Lord. They're mean, cantankerous, rude, prideful, live however they see fit, and are often very unapproachable. We need prophets in the land like Samuel, of whom the Bible declares, **"None of his words fell to the ground."** This is why the prophet Samuel commanded the attention of many others who sensed the call in this office. Samuel had a revelation of the Word, and I believe a revelation of worship. He had a revelation of serving in the temple, and attending to the things of the Lord. He was also found faithful in another man's domain, that of Eli. Samuel had:

- The **Scriptures**
- **Stability**
- A **Servant's heart**
- **Familiarity** with the **Sanctuary**
- **Familiarity** with the **Supernatural**
- A **Sensitivity** to the **Spirit of God**
- He was **Above Suspicion**.

Real prophets demonstrate the heart of the Father and the spirit of boldness, and they understand that the prophetic gift is for the greater good of others and not for themselves. There is a need for real prophets in the land. Prophets with the eyes in the spirit to see like Isaiah, (the "eagle eye" prophet), and prophets like Obadiah, who expressed a real heart for protecting the office and the gift of the prophetic. We need prophets like Elijah and Elisha, those who were willing to stand up for God and move in supernatural miracles. Elijah moved in sixteen recorded miracles and his protégé, Elisha, moved in thirty-two miracles. We need to see the prophets of God arise like never before in the Body of Christ. Prophets who go against the grain. Who live on the edge. Who are willing to go to what are often hard-to-describe places to the average believer. Who are attuned to the Spirit of God. Their ears are always found listening to the voice of God. As I often say, "God is always *speaking*... we're just not always *listening*."

Real prophets know that when God starts speaking, we open our mouths; but when He stops, we shut them! Plain and simple!

Prophets stand for truth and justice. Prophets are the ones who come from a place of the spirit vs. the profits, who come from a place in the soul. The truth is that the church is full of prophets and prophetic gifts who are led by their own souls instead of the Spirit of God.

Your soul consists of several components: your mind, your will, your emotions, your intellect, and your imagination. Your prophetic gift will be led by either your soul or by the Spirit of God.

The question has been asked, "Should prophets be planted?" I'm going to say yes. I believe that ministry gifts who serve in the office of the prophet should be planted or have some sort of covering. This can be a sensitive subject and it is not often confronted. Prophets who hear the voice of God also need to hear order, submission, and accountability. This should not be for the purpose of controlling them, because ultimately, they answer to God. There is an order that I believe the Lord has put in place to govern and guide His ministry gifts.

Let's look at a particular Scripture for the sake of argument. The Bible tells us that **"Those who are planted in the house of the Lord shall flourish in the courts of our God. They shall still bear fruit in old age; they shall be fresh and flourishing." Psalm 92:13-14 (NKJV)**

In this passage, the will of the Lord for His people is clearly stated. It is for them to be planted in His house—to have roots in a particular local church. The word **planted** means "to be stationary or permanent." When something is planted, it does not move around. It is in a fixed location.

The Scripture promised us that those who are planted will flourish. The word **flourish** is defined as "To break forth as a bud." In other words—*breakthrough*! Those who are planted will have *breakthrough* in their lives.

*Flourish* is also defined as "to blossom and to spread."

Nothing blossoms without being planted. Planting is the *prerequisite for the satisfying of God's promise*.

The church has had enough of "Nomadic Prophets." Wanderers, or people who think that they are "all that." A nomad is a person who often shifts from one place to another. They are wanderers... people without a permanent home. They often follow a traditional circuit according to the state of the pasturage or food supply. We see this in the prophetic ministry where prophets come in, blow up, and blow out. We have seen when they have gone from place to place, and have no base to take off from or anywhere to land. It is a scary place to be for ministries who are desperate for the Word of the Lord to just have anyone who calls themselves a "prophet" to minister to their flock. My take on this is that if they're *not planted,* then they're *not in order*.

So many pastors and churches have been destroyed because they thought they were getting a Prophet, when they actually got a Profit! Another question is this—if they're not planted, who are they tithing to? Let me just share a word of wisdom to the pastors and leaders out there. I get it. I know you want your church to grow, you want God to manifest the prophetic, to increase and walk in and under an open Heaven. But you must be wise and discerning.

A couple of years ago, some friends of ours were deceived by a "fly by night" apostle and his wife. They emptied out their savings when this so-called "apostle" told them that "The Lord said for you to come under me and pay tithes to me." And in the midst of all of this mess, he told them that he had heard the Lord say, "We are to have a conference at the convention center and you're supposed to put up the money." The apostle told her that God was going to fill the place. When the time came, no one showed up but them. I believe they lost their deposit, or part of it. This out-of-town apostle moved into their city and took most of the people who had been a part of this couple's ministry.

After talking with them over the phone, I told them that this didn't sound right from the beginning. I don't know you and you don't know me… but watch this! When a person is desperate for belonging, or just longing for fellowship, it is easy to get on the radar of "spiritual foxes." It was a lesson learned.

There was also a pastor and his wife in the same city who this couple referred to me, because they had let a female prophet from out-of-town come into their house for over two weeks, for some sort of revival. This lady sowed "prophetic weed seeds" throughout the congregation and nearly destroyed the legacy of this pastor's church. The same thing I shared with the first couple I shared with them, "You must *inspect* what you *expect*."

Not being planted often leads to error and divination, which are, by the way, becoming more and more common in the prophetic ministry. I'm not saying that this applies to everyone, because there may be some unusual situations. But at the end of day, order is order, and a prophet cannot guide you effectively if he or she has not had some sort of planting in their lives.

**Elisha** was planted in the life of **Elijah**... **Joshua** was planted in the life of **Moses**... **David** was even planted in a house where he eventually had to run for his life! In the New Testament, you have **Timothy, Titus,** and **Philemon**, all of whom were planted in the life of the **Apostle Paul**, and the **Twelve Disciples** who were planted in the life of **Jesus**. This is a pattern that is followed throughout the Scriptures.

Let's not be so *prophetic* that we become *pathetic* and miss out of the promises and the positioning of God.

When I'm planted...

- I'm **patient**
- I'm in the **process**
- I'm in **pursuit** of something
- I'm **proving** to myself, God, and others that I can do this
- I'm involved in **prayer**
- I'm engaged in **praise** and **worship**

"Believe me, woman, the time is coming when you Samaritans will worship the Father neither here at this mountain nor there in Jerusalem. You worship guessing in the dark; we Jews worship in the clear light of day. God's way of salvation is made available through the Jews. But the time is coming—it has, in fact, come—when what you're called will not matter and where you go to worship will not matter. It's who you are and the way you live that count before God. Your worship must engage your spirit in the pursuit of truth. That's the kind of people the Father is out looking for: those who are simply and honestly themselves before him in their worship. God is sheer being itself—Spirit. Those who worship him must do it out of their very being, their spirits, their true selves, in adoration. It's who you are and the way you live that count before God. *Your worship must engage your spirit in the pursuit of truth*. That's the kind of people the Father is looking for: those who are simply and honestly *themselves* before him in their worship. God is sheer being Himself—Spirit. Those who worship him must do it out of their very being, their spirits, their true selves, in adoration." John 4:23-24 (MSG)

*"True worship will divert the spirit of error."*

**Divert**: "to cause (someone or something) to change course or turn from one direction to another."

God tells us His view of divination in **Deuteronomy 18:10**: **"There shall not be found among you...anyone who practices divination or tells fortunes or interprets omens."**

**1 Samuel 15:10** compares rebellion to the sin of divination. One of the reasons there is such an increase in the spirit of error as it relates to the prophetic, is because of the lack of spiritual effort to mature in this area.

**Divination** is defined as "The practice of seeking knowledge of the future or the unknown by supernatural means." According to english.stackexchange.com, the etymology of "Div" is used in the context of displaying stupidity, or a foolish person. In the church, divination is when the nation of darkness attempts to overthrow and substitute itself for the nation of light. It's a form of godlessness with the appearance of a spiritual component. It is associated with the occult and involves fortune-telling or "soothsaying," as it used to be called. It thrives in an environment of Ahab being present! It streams from a spirit of error! Error has to do with wrong judgment and conduct. The assignment of this spirit ultimately is to dislocate, disassemble, disfigure, and divorce you from the presence of God and His Word.

This is the enemy's stance, and he is stupid to think he can overpower or replace the King of Kings! I declare it's time as ministry gifts that we release the Spirit of Truth instead of the Spirit of Error.

**"Beloved, believe not every spirit, but try the spirits whether they are of God: because many false prophets are gone out into the world. Hereby know ye the Spirit of God: Every spirit that confesseth that Jesus Christ is come in the flesh is of God: And every spirit that confesseth not that Jesus Christ is come in the flesh is not of God: and this is that spirit of antichrist, whereof ye have heard that it should come; and even now already is it in the world. Ye are of God, little children, and have overcome them: because greater is he that is in you, than he that is in the world. They are of the world: therefore, speak they of the world, and the world heareth them. We are of God: he that knoweth God heareth us; he that is not of God heareth not us. Hereby know we the spirit of truth, and the spirit of error." 1 John 4:1-6 (KJV)**

This is a subject that is not discussed very often in the prophetic ministry, perhaps because some may be operating in it either intentionally or unintentionally. It is a "counterfeit and unencrypted currency" of the prophetic ministry. When the prophetic is encrypted, it's protected from potential hacking and hijacking. You encrypt it by studying the Word, staying in a place of worship and holiness, and leaning not to your own understanding and interpretation.

**"Trust in the Lord with all thine heart; and lean not unto thine own understanding. In all thy ways acknowledge him, and he shall direct thy paths." Proverbs 3:5-6 (KJV)**

Here is one of the most relevant examples of someone who was off and influenced by a spirit that was not the Spirit of the Lord.

**"Once when we were going to the place of prayer, we were met by a female slave who had a spirit by which she predicted the future. She earned a great deal of money for her owners by fortune-telling. She followed Paul and the rest of us, shouting, 'These men are servants of the Most High God, who are telling you the way to be saved.' She kept this up for many days. Finally, Paul became so annoyed that he turned around and said to the spirit, 'In the name of Jesus Christ I command you to come out of her!' At that moment, the spirit left her. When her owners realized that their hope of making money was gone, they seized Paul and Silas and dragged them into the marketplace to face the authorities. They brought them before the magistrates and said, 'These men are Jews, and are throwing our city into an uproar by advocating customs unlawful for us Romans to accept or practice.'" Acts 16:16-21 (NIV)**

What I have discovered is that what people do not understand, they criticize. The prophetic nature and the spiritual gifts of God are for the benefit or advancement of the Kingdom of God and equipping the saints.

Two relevant questions to ask: "How long are the prophets going to be needed in the church?" and "Were they just for the Old Testament and not the New Testament?" To answer them, let's look at what the Apostle Paul said in **Ephesians 4:10-16**. There are so many opinions about the prophets, and the gifts of the Spirit, that many just don't bother to investigate the matter further. I want to assure you, though, that we need the true prophets of God more than we ever have in the Body of Christ.

**"He who descended is the very same as He who also has ascended high above all the heavens, that He [His presence] might fill all things [that is, the whole universe]). And [His gifts to the church were varied and] He Himself appointed some as apostles [special messengers, representatives], some as prophets [who speak a new message from God to the people], some as evangelists [who spread the good news of salvation], and some as pastors and teachers [to shepherd and guide and instruct], [and He did this] to fully equip and perfect the saints (God's people) for works of service, to build up the body of Christ [the church]; until we all reach oneness in the faith and in the knowledge of the Son of God, [growing spiritually] to become a mature believer, reaching to the measure of the fullness of Christ [manifesting His spiritual completeness and exercising our spiritual gifts in unity]. So that we are no longer children [spiritually immature], tossed back and forth [like ships on a stormy sea] and carried about by every wind of [shifting] doctrine, by the cunning and trickery of [unscrupulous] men, by the deceitful scheming of people ready to do anything [for personal profit]. But speaking the truth in love [in all**

**things—both our speech and our lives expressing His truth], let us grow up in all things into Him [following His example] who is the Head—Christ. From Him the whole body [the church, in all its various parts], joined and knitted firmly together by what every joint supplies, when each part is working properly, causes the body to grow and mature, building itself up in [unselfish] love." Ephesians 4:10-16 (AMP)**

Prophets that flourish in the gifts and assignments don't just have the knowledge which is the "know of" but they also have the wisdom, which is the "do of."

**"Wisdom is the principal thing; Therefore get wisdom. And in all your getting, get understanding. Exalt her, and she will promote you; she will bring you honor, when you embrace her. She will place on your head an ornament of grace; a crown of glory she will deliver to you." Proverbs 4:7 (NIV)**

The prophetic flow is simply "inspiration and revelation released by His grace." It is a special endowment of the Holy Spirit to assist and aid you in reaching and maximizing your full potential in God. I believe that when the church begins to see this as a whole, then we will experience another dimension of the Spirit of God.

Prophecy, or prophesying, is simply "a discourse (speech) emanating from divine inspiration and declaring the purposes of God, whether by reproving and admonishing the wicked, comforting the afflicted, or revealing things hidden." It's not just the *foretelling* that which is "*stating what the future will hold before it happens,*" but it's the *forthtelling* as well, "*that which is proclaiming the truth.*"

There are so many people who don't understand the spirit of prophecy. I believe that this has caused an issue in the prophetic ministry. People often use prophesy and prophecy in the wrong context. Notice here, at the end of the word *prophecy* is the word that sounds like the word *"see,"* "to be able to look in the spirit realm." In the word *prophesy*, at the end of this word is the word that sounds like *"sigh," "to pause, consider, and weigh out before you open your mouth."* I believe even in this simple yet profound example, when it comes to delivering a prophetic word, we must learn to be patient in prophecy to get in the position to prophesy. Prophecy requires knowledge and patience, it requires understanding; and when there is a degree of understanding, you can then prophesy.

I have a simple acronym for the word prophecy that I'd like to share with you.

**PROPHECY: P**ower **R**eleased in **O**peration with **P**urpose and **H**eaven's **E**ncounter of **C**hange for **Y**ou!

When prophecy is delivered, and you are the recipient, you can do one of two things: either accept it or reject it! Just because everyone calls themselves a prophet does not mean that you have to receive a word from them. I have found out that when prophecies don't come to pass, it is not always an indication that the individual is a false prophet. Faith can be a factor, or it could be an undisclosed area of someone's life pertaining to sin or simply just not being obedient.

> *"Prophecy is not automatic, and it is contingent upon obedience, faith, and your submission to His will for your life."*

For those of you who hunger for more Scriptures with the word *prophecy* in them, I have taken the liberty of assisting you in this endeavor. The word *prophecy* is referenced at least twenty-one times in the King James Version of the Bible. These are found in **Appendix A** at the end of this book.

It is important to some extent that you know of those who are in ministry. I'm not saying that you have to know their mother and father, where they live, and what they drive. The fact is you may not be able to know them all personally. But for those that you do have the honor of getting to know, it is very important to know their fruit, especially when we are in such a society where up is down, out is in, right is left, and bad is good. There is so much that goes on in the church circuit these days that you must have a life of discernment and prayer. Just because everything *sounds good* doesn't necessarily mean it's good *for you*.

One of the ways you can discern someone's prophetic gift is simply to "track their truth." Does it measure up with the Word of God? Are they standing upon the Scriptures? Are they glorifying God in the midst of it? Are they in fellowship with a reputable covering? Does their prophetic gift draw your attention towards God? When it comes down to it, you have the permission of Heaven to be a fruit inspector! *Check the fruit* before you take it home or take it to heart.

**"Let two or three prophets speak [as inspired by the Holy Spirit], while the rest pay attention and weigh carefully what is said." 1 Corinthians 14:29 (AMP)**

The Bible is our template and road map to assist us in this endeavor. We make our life rather arduous at times because we don't know how to judge prophecy and say, "No that's not it!"

There are Scriptures to help validate this statement.

- *It should build up or help construct the body of believers:* **"One who speaks in a tongue edifies himself; but one who prophesies edifies the church [promotes growth in spiritual wisdom, devotion, holiness, and joy]." 1 Corinthians 14:4 (AMP)**

- *It should be in agreement with the Word:* **"But evil men and impostors will go on from bad to worse, deceiving and being deceived. But as for you, continue in the things that you have learned and of which you are convinced [holding tightly to the truths], knowing from whom you learned them, and how from childhood you have known the sacred writings (Hebrew Scriptures) which are able to give you the wisdom that leads to salvation through faith which is in Christ Jesus [surrendering your entire self to Him and having absolute confidence in His wisdom, power and goodness]. All Scripture is God-breathed [given by divine inspiration] and is profitable for instruction, for conviction [of sin], for correction [of error and restoration to obedience], for training in righteousness [learning to live in conformity to God's will, both publicly and privately—behaving honorably with personal integrity and moral courage]; so that the man of God may be complete and proficient, outfitted and thoroughly equipped for every good work." 2 Timothy 3:16 (AMP)**

- *It should always exalt Jesus, not you:* **"But when He, the Spirit of Truth, comes, He will guide you into all the truth [full and complete truth]. For He will not speak on His own initiative, but He will speak whatever He hears [from the Father—the message regarding the Son], and He will disclose to you what is to come [in the future]. He will glorify and** honor me, because He (the Holy Spirit) will take from what is mine and will disclose it to you." John 16:13-14 (AMP)

*"I decree and declare that prophetic balance will release a wind of prophetic strength. Prophetic strength releases **Stamina**, a sense of **Security**, **Supply**, and **Structure**. It's a **Source**. It defies the realm of the **Senses**. It releases a **Surge**. It will cause you to **Soar**, **Spring forth** and **Spread out** in Jesus' name."*

- *It should come to pass:* **"When a prophet speaks in the name of the Lord and the thing does not happen or come true, that is the thing which the Lord has not spoken. The prophet has spoken it presumptuously; you shall not be afraid of him." Deuteronomy 18:22 (AMP)**

- *It should always lead to Jehovah and obedience to Him:* **"If a prophet arises among you, or a dreamer of dreams, and gives you a sign or a wonder, and the sign or the wonder which he spoke (foretold) to you comes to pass, and if he says, 'Let us follow after other gods (whom you have not known) and let us serve and worship them,' you shall not listen to the words of that prophet or that dreamer of dreams; for the Lord your God is testing you to know whether you love the Lord your God with all your heart and mind and all your soul [your entire being]. You shall walk after the Lord your God and you shall fear [and worship] Him [with awe-filled reverence and profound respect], and you shall keep His commandments and you shall listen to His voice, and you shall serve Him, and cling to Him. But that prophet or that dreamer of dreams shall be put to death, because he has counseled rebellion against the Lord your God who brought you from the land of Egypt and redeemed you from the** house of slavery, to draw you away from the way in which the Lord your God has commanded you to walk. So, you shall remove the evil from among you." Deuteronomy 13:1-5 (AMP)

- *It should produce freedom in your life:* **"For you have not received a spirit of slavery leading again to fear [of God's judgment], but you have received the Spirit of adoption as sons [the Spirit producing sonship] by which we [joyfully] cry, "Abba! Father!" The Spirit Himself testifies and confirms together with our spirit [assuring us] that we [believers] are children of God. And if [we are His] children, [then we are His] heirs also: heirs of God and fellow heirs with Christ [sharing His spiritual blessing and inheritance], if indeed we share in His suffering so that we may also share in His glory." Romans 8:15-17 (AMP)**

- *It should produce life:* **"He has qualified us [making us sufficient] as ministers of a new covenant [of salvation through Christ], not of the letter [of a written code] but of the Spirit; for the letter [of the Law] kills [by revealing sin and demanding obedience], but the Spirit gives life." 2 Corinthians 3:6 (AMP)**

A prophet's primary function in the Old Testament was to serve as God's representative, mouthpiece, voice, spokesman or spokeswoman, and ambassador, by communicating and delivering God's word to His people. Authentic prophets never spoke on their own will, volition, and authority or shared their personal opinions and perspectives, but delivered the message or messages God gave them. There are several references that validate this statement.

**"So, we have the prophetic word made more certain. You do well to pay [close] attention to it as to a lamp**

shining in a dark place, until the day dawns and light breaks through the gloom and the morning star arises in your hearts. But understand this first of all, that no prophecy of Scripture is a matter of or comes from one's own [personal or special] interpretation, for no prophecy was ever made by an act of human will, but men moved by the Holy Spirit spoke from God." 2 Peter 1:19-21 (AMP)

Here are several prophets that the Lord spoke to: Moses, Jeremiah, and Ezekiel were just a few.

"'Now then go, and I, even I, will be with your mouth, and will teach you what you shall say.' God assured Moses, 'I will raise up for [my people] a prophet like you son...'" Exodus 4:12 (AMP)

"I will raise up a prophet from among their countrymen like you, and I will put My words in his mouth, and he shall speak to them all that I command him. It shall come about that whoever will not listen to My words which he shall speak in My name, I Myself will require it of him [and there will be consequences]. But the prophet who presumes to speak a word in My name which I have not commanded him to speak, or which he speaks in the name of other gods—that prophet shall die.' If you say in your heart, 'How will we know and recognize the word which the Lord has not spoken?' When a prophet speaks in the name of the Lord and the thing does not happen or come true, that is the thing which the Lord has not spoken. The prophet has spoken it presumptuously; you shall not be afraid of him." Deuteronomy 18:18-21 (AMP)

"Then the Lord stretched out His hand and touched my mouth, and the Lord said to me, 'Behold (hear Me), I have put My words in your mouth.'" Jeremiah 1:9 (AMP)

**"But you shall speak my words to them whether they will listen or refuse [to listen], for they are [most] rebellious. As for you, son of man, listen to what I say to you; do not be rebellious like that rebellious house; open your mouth and eat what I am giving you." Ezekiel 2:7-8 (AMP)**

If you take notice that whenever the Bible begins to reference the prophets of God in the Old Testament, it was most likely preceded by the expressed statement and then the Word of the Lord came. It was not about their agenda, what they wanted or even their desires. It was the Word of the Lord that came and will always be. I love how the prophet Isaiah crystallizes this text:

**"For My thoughts are not your thoughts, Nor are your ways My ways,' declares the Lord. 'For as the heavens are higher than the earth, So are My ways higher than your ways And My thoughts higher than your thoughts. For as the rain and snow come down from heaven, And do not return there without watering the earth, Making it bear and sprout, And providing seed to the sower and bread to the eater, So will My word be which goes out of My mouth; It will not return to Me void (useless, without result), Without accomplishing what I desire, And without succeeding in the matter for which I sent it." Isaiah 55:8-11 (AMP)**

Let me close with this: True *prophets* will always set the stage for *God* to get the glory, and true *profits* will always set the stage for *themselves* to get the glory!

*Chapter 8*

# THE THREAD OF THE PROPHETIC

**Fellowship, Covenantship, Relationship, and Mentorship**

*"As prophetic ministry gifts, we must learn the logistics and the laws of the prophetic so that we can operate in it with longevity and integrity."*

*"To be prophetic is to be different... not weird."*

Let me just start here by saying that the underlying thread of the prophetic is the Holy Spirit. The Bible tells us that after we've received the gift of the Holy Spirit, we shall have power.

**"But you will receive power when the Holy Spirit comes on you; and you will be my witnesses in Jerusalem, and in all Judea and Samaria, and to the ends of the earth." Acts 1:8 (NIV)**

The interesting thing about the prophetic gift is that in order for it to be active and flowing in your life, there must be a connection with the Holy Spirit. If you intend to function in this area of ministry, then it is important to be led by the Spirit of God.

**"The Spirit of truth. The world cannot accept him, because it neither sees him nor knows him. But you know him, for he lives with you and will be in you." John 14:17 (NIV)**

**"But when he, the Spirit of truth, comes, he will guide you into all the truth. He will not speak on his own; he will speak only what he hears, and he will tell you what is yet to come." John 16:13 (NIV)**

One of the first things I want to discuss here is that of the word **fellowship**. According to Merriam –Webster, *fellowship* is "meaningful communication for building trust and fellowship." It also means "to develop a partnership or companionship." The Greek word here, **Koinonia,** can therefore refer in some contexts to a jointly contributed gift. The word appears nineteen times in most editions of the Greek New Testament. In the New American Standard Bible, it translated *fellowship* twelve times, *sharing* three times, and *participation* and *contribution* twice each.

**"No one has ever seen God, but the one and only Son, who is himself God and is in closest relationship with the Father, has made him known." John 1:18 (NIV)**

Fellowship in this part of the prophetic thread involves *daily devotion, fasting, consecration,* and *isolation*. Time spent with the Father allows you to recognize His voice… and Him to recognize yours. Some people don't invest the time needed to learn His voice.

I often say, *"When I discern, I learn."* Learning His voice will not happen automatically. It won't happen by impartation, and it won't happen by hands being laid on you. It won't happen by going to every seminar or conference that there is. I learn His voice through the *time I personally invest*. For instance, I cannot expect a withdrawal from my checking account if there is nothing there to withdraw from. One of the sad things I've noticed about the prophetic is that too many prophetic voices depend more on the grace that accompanies the assignment than on spending time in His presence! You can sharpen your ear to hear the voice of the Lord as you spend more intimate time with Him. The Holy Spirit longs to fellowship with us daily, not just once a week, or when we have to preach!

**"For those who are led by the Spirit of God are the children of God." Romans 8:14 (NIV)**

The word **covenant** means "a formal, solemn, and binding agreement between two or more persons to do, or not to do, something specified."

The Hebrew word for covenant, **Berith,** has to do with "being allies" or "binding between God and man." The Greek word **Diatheke**, usually translated *covenant* in English versions of the Bible, is a legal term denoting "a formal and legally binding declaration of benefits to be given by one party to another, with or without conditions attached." The word *covenant* occurs 342 times in 313 verses in the NIV, emphasizing how important covenant is to the Lord.

One of the most powerful things about the thread of the prophetic is what it releases in one's life when one is in agreement with the Word, God's timing, and the Spirit of God. God tells us even in His Word that when we are in covenant with Him, we will have access to His promises. When it comes down to the prophetic, the greater your submission to Him, the stronger the flow of the prophetic gift will be in your life.

The best place to be in is a place of grace and favor. It's when your character is placed before your gift, when your attitude or disposition is leveled and centered, when you walk in compassion and wisdom and because of your link to Him, that He will always want to use your gift. Why? *Because it's for His glory!*

Coming to know the Lord was the best decision of my life. Surrendering my gift to Him never ceases to amaze me, especially when I witness the lives of people being tremendously blessed. One thing I have learned to be so true is that you can't put a price on this!

Remaining in covenant with the Father will release another level of prophetic ministry that will blow your mind. Remember that He's always to be at the center as we minister as prophetic gifts.

Another thread of the prophetic is **Relationship**. *Relationship* is "The state of being related or interrelated. A state of affairs existing between those having relations or dealings."

**"You must worship no other gods, for the LORD, whose very name is Jealous, is a God who is jealous about his relationship with you." Exodus 34:14 (NLT)**

As a younger minister, I didn't realize how much of a religious spirit I was under. What is a religious spirit? Simply put, it is "a spirit that is committed to convenience."

There was a time when I was growing in the things of God, and I thought I was good. As my relationship with the Lord began to develop, my appetite changed. One of things I think I did, as I believe many others have done, is based my salvation on what a person was saying or telling me. One of the craziest things I've discovered is that *the same God who has anointed the men and women of God is the One who can anoint me!* I had to learn to stop living *for others* and *through others.* Many people get trapped in this place, and they go through life bound, restricted and limited. Many believers are trapped in a *religionship* and have yet to experience a *relationship* with the Father.

**"But mark this: There will be terrible times in the last days. People will be lovers of themselves, lovers of**

money, boastful, proud, abusive, disobedient to their parents, ungrateful, unholy, without love, unforgiving, slanderous, without self-control, brutal, not lovers of the good, treacherous, rash, conceited, lovers of pleasure rather than lovers of God—having a form of godliness but denying its power. Have nothing to do with such people." 2 Timothy 3:1-5 (NIV)

"Anyone who wanders away from this teaching has no relationship with God. But anyone who remains in the teaching of Christ has a relationship with both the Father and the Son." 2 John 1:9 (NLT)

**Mentorship** is simply "allowing someone the opportunity to journey through life with you until you reach your prophetic destiny."

There are other dynamics of the prophetic thread that I must expound on as well. For instance:

- **Currency**: "The quality or state of being current." It has to do with the *circulation* of the prophetic.
- **Fluency**: "Capable of moving like a liquid or involving minimal difficulty or effort." Synonyms of fluent include eloquent, articulate, silver-tongued, and well-spoken. It has to do with the *consistency* of the prophetic.
- **Accuracy**: "Freedom from mistake or error and conformity to truth or to a standard or model." Accuracy has to do with the specific, rather than the general, aspects of prophecy, and also the pure *connection* to the Holy Spirit.
- **Character**: "Moral excellence and firmness. A characteristic property that defines the apparent individual nature of something." Character has to do with the *conformity* of the prophetic.

The thread of the prophetic that holds it all together is, of course, the Holy Spirit. Here are just a few more things to consider and be aware of:

- **Humility**
- **Honor**
- **Hope**
- **Hearing**
- **Hands-on Training**

*Chapter 9*

# UNDERSTANDING THE MANTLE

*"Humility is a vital key to walking under a mantle associated with the office of the prophet."*

A **mantle**, according to the Merriam-Webster Dictionary, is "a figurative cloak symbolizing preeminence or authority," or "something that covers, enfolds, or envelops." This can be interpreted from the external, or natural, perspective. However, I believe this is just one aspect of the mantle. There is also an internal or spiritual component as well, and this is the other aspect that I would like you to consider, which is relative to leadership. When character is in place, it validates the calling and the assignment of the office.

> *The mantle is that which is initiated by God. It is the containment of the supernatural of a man or woman of God. It is the capacity to carry an anointing of authority in an office or position. It's the disposition. The covering or the mantle is revealed and released through a revelation of the Scriptures through fasting and prayer and most importantly, discipline.*

Elijah, the prophet, was under a mantle. He knew how important it was to operate under an unprecedented level of grace, and he knew that to do so, he had to stay under the mantle. Samuel the prophet, of whom the Bible declares "none of his words fell to the ground," knew the secret to his success as a prophet was to conform to the Word of God.

You may have not heard this before, but I need you to hear it now, by the Spirit of the Lord. When you actually weigh out several things here, we see that the mantle comes with a level of maturity, not just a desire to "be in the ministry." I have seen many prophets and prophetic ministry gifts who are all about the ministry, but lack maturity. This has become a major epidemic in the Body of Christ. We now have prophets in some circles who are accepted based on their gifts, and not their fruits!

The Bible declares,

**"No good tree bears bad fruit, nor does a bad tree bear good fruit. Each tree is recognized by its own fruit. People do not pick figs from thorn bushes, or grapes from briars. A good man brings good things out of the good stored up in his heart, and an evil man brings evil things out of the evil stored up in his heart. For the mouth speaks what the heart is full of." Luke 6:43-45 (NIV)**

It's amazing how everyone tries to make the prophet and the mantle the same. When you look through Scripture, you will discover that when a prophet walked in a heavy prophet flow, it was because they had been tried in the fire. They had been proven. They had tied themselves up in the Scriptures, and prayed, fasted, and worshipped often.

In the times we're living in now, you don't find many people in prayer, because we have become conditioned to relying on the grace that accompanies the office. We have become *presentation*-driven as opposed to *presence*-driven. As prophetic gifts to the body, it is so needed for us as prophets and prophetic presbytery, to stay focused and centered on the things of God.

The Bible states that there are three things that drive people that are "in the world."

**"The lust of the eye, the lust of the flesh and the pride of life." 1 John 2:16 (NIV)**

Think about this! If you have an umbrella, the purpose of it is to keep you covered from the elements in the environment. If by chance, you relocate from under the umbrella, you will now be subject to what is happening around you. Wisdom says that if I don't want to get wet, then I must stay under the covering of the umbrella. It's the same principle when it comes to the mantle. We must learn that you only remain safe if you do it God's way, and not your way.

**"There is a way that appears to be right, but in the end, it leads to death." Proverbs 16:25 (NIV)**

Sometimes, people or prophetic gifts will miss out on walking under the mantle, because they have been misguided, have unrealistic expectations, are guilty of not counting up the cost or have misinterpreted their gift.

What I'm saying is that the two are separate. You don't just "wake up" and have a prophet's mantle. It is something that develops over a period of time. I often say that prophets are not made overnight, or in a week, or a month... not even in a year. We are forever evolving and becoming more like Jesus as we pursue Him.

The *office* of the prophet and the *mantle* of the prophet are two distinct things that work together to accomplish the plan of God. The office of the prophet is the *Assignment* and the mantle of the prophet is the *Alignment*.

**MANTLE:**

- **M**erges with the message of His Word
- **A**ssumes nothing about his or her assignment
- (The) **N**ataph and **N**abi grace is stronger
- **T**enure: they have the right and authority to release the Word of the Lord
- **L**ongs for truth and justice
- **E**lbow—the joint that connects us to God, and to our destiny

Here is just an overview of some of the prophets that stood out in the Bible:

## Old Testament Major Prophets

Isaiah
Jeremiah
Ezekiel
Daniel
Habakkuk
Zephaniah
Haggai
Zechariah
Malachi

## Minor Prophets

Hosea
Joel
Amos
Obadiah
Jonah
Micah
Nahum

## Other Prophets

Elijah
Elisha
Gad
Micaiah
Nathan
Samuel

## New Testament Prophets

John the Baptist
John the Revelator
Agubus
Anna
Barnabas
Paul the Apostle

*Chapter 10*

# THE "THREE P'S" OF THE PROPHETIC

*"True prophets and 5-fold ministry gifts are not led by **P**opularity, **P**eople, **P**ersonalities, **P**ropositions or **P**ressure; they are led by God's **P**resence and His **P**urpose."*

**Purity**

Purity is a subject that most people in the church are quiet about these days, but just like gold has to be purified from impurities in order to release its value, so it is with the prophetic. It is important that when we release the Word of the Lord, that it is birthed from our *spirit* and not our *soul*. We cannot afford to allow the influences of the world to twist and pervert the prophetic Word of the Lord. There are so many things that the world has to offer, but there is no substitute for purity. Purity is something you can't be forced to have; it has to be a life choice. Our Bishop, I. V. Hilliard always says, "Life is not desire or wish-driven, it's *choice*-driven."

**"But if serving the LORD seems undesirable to you, then choose for yourselves this day whom you will serve, whether the gods your ancestors served beyond the Euphrates, or the gods of the Amorites, in whose land you are living. But as for me and my household, we will serve the LORD." Joshua 24:15 (NIV)**

"It is God's will that you should be sanctified: that you should avoid sexual immorality; that each of you should learn to control your own body in a way that is holy and honorable, not in passionate lust like the pagans, who do not know God…" 1 Thessalonians 4:3-5 (NIV)

"Don't let anyone look down on you because you are young, but set an example for the believers in speech, in conduct, in love, in faith and in purity." 1 Timothy 4:12 (NIV)

"How can a young person stay on the path of purity? By living according to your word." Psalms 119:9 (NIV)

"We put no stumbling block in anyone's path, so that our ministry will not be discredited. Rather, as servants of God we commend ourselves in every way: in great endurance; in troubles, hardships and distresses; in beatings, imprisonments and riots; in hard work, sleepless nights and hunger; in purity, understanding, patience and kindness; in the Holy Spirit and in sincere love; in truthful speech and in the power of God; with weapons of righteousness in the right hand and in the left; through glory and dishonor, bad report and good report; genuine, yet regarded as impostors; known, yet regarded as unknown; dying, and yet we live on; beaten, and yet not killed; sorrowful, yet always rejoicing; poor, yet making many rich; having nothing, and yet possessing everything." 2 Corinthians 6:3-10 (NIV)

"Create in me a pure heart, O God, and renew a steadfast spirit within me. Do not cast me from your presence or take your Holy Spirit from me. Restore to me the joy of your salvation and grant me a willing spirit, to sustain me." Psalm 51:10-12 (NIV)

## Passion

*"The proof and evidence of your passion is revealed in your relentless pursuit of Him."*

**"Whatever you do, work at it with all your heart, as working for the Lord, not for human masters..." Colossians 3:23 (NIV)**

**"It teaches us to say 'No' to ungodliness and worldly passions, and to live self-controlled, upright and godly lives in this present age..." Titus 2:12 (NIV)**

Passion is *power*. Passion is an *excessive and uncommon desire.* It is *magnetic*, and *unforgettable*. There are several things that I have learned about passion. One of the most important things that I've learned is that you must, *at any cost*, protect your passion! When you're passionate about something, you mustn't allow people to distract, deter, discourage or detour you from your prophetic destiny! Yes, child of God, *you have a destiny*! What exactly is a destiny, you may ask? According to the dictionary, it is "the fixed order of things; invincible necessity; fate; and irresistible power or agency conceived of as determining the future, whether in general or of an individual."

It is your responsibility to protect it and walk it out! Because when you have a prophetic destiny, *you have to go through the process of elimination to prepare for elevation*. What does this look like?

- **Disconnection** of certain people from your life
- **Deliverance** from a religious mindset
- **Freedom** from people's opinions of you and the willingness and availability to allow God to stretch you out of your comfort zone!

As I often say, ***nothing great ever comes out of a comfort zone!*** David was a great example of one who was passionate about his purpose. The Bible references him as a man after the heart of God. David was a true worshipper!

**Purpose**

The prophetic is, in essence, "the flow or demonstration of the prophecy led and inspired by the Holy Spirit."

**"But it is the spirit in a person, the breath of the Almighty that gives them understanding." Job 32:8 (NIV)**

One of the most amazing things I've learned in this season of my life is to *walk in my purpose to the best of my ability*. Walking in my purpose is more than just being about me; it's about positioning myself to be a *blessing* and *impact the body of Christ and with the prophetic ministry*. I believe it grieves the heart of the Father to see His sons and daughters not carrying out their purpose on the earth. Out of over seven billion people on this planet, many of them are just here, merely existing and not living. One of the greatest revelations I've received is that life is not *determined* by you but *discovered* by you. The prophetic ministry is what started me on this unbelievable journey to walking in my assignment.

We must never forget that the prophetic ministry is not to be mistaken for a game, or used to make a name for yourself, or to acquire fame.

> *The purpose of the prophetic ministry is to tap into those areas of your life that activate and awaken you. They provoke and prepare you to navigate and release fresh revelation. You need to stir up the wells that have been dried up by religion and opposing forces, and find clarity and confirmation concerning your assignment.*

That which is misunderstood can be subject to abuse. There has been so much perversion and twisting of the prophetic that people are turned off by it—almost frightened, if you will. I believe though, without a doubt, that there is a new breed of prophetic ministry gifts that are rising in this hour—those that will lean into their prophetic assignment and guard that gift with their life.

**"But I have raised you up for this very purpose, that I might show you my power and that my name might be proclaimed in all the earth." Exodus 9:16 (NIV)**

**"God is mighty, but despises no one; he is mighty, and firm in his purpose." Job 36:5 (NIV)**

**"But the plans of the LORD stand firm forever, the purposes of his heart through all generations." Psalms 33:11 (NIV)**

**"Many are the plans in a person's heart, but it is the LORD's purpose that prevails." Proverbs 19:21 (NIV)**

**"The purposes of a person's heart are deep waters, but one who has insight draws them out." Proverbs 20:5 (NIV)**

**"So is my word that goes out from my mouth: It will not return to me empty, but will accomplish what I desire and achieve the purpose for which I sent it." Isaiah 55:11 (NIV)**

Now because we have just briefly touched on the three P's of the Prophetic, let me also note here that there are at least twenty-one or so references to the word *prophecy* in the KJV. Here is a list of Scriptures that relate to prophecy:

### The Burden of the Lord

*"The heavier the burden of the Lord is on the life of the prophet, the higher the Lord will elevate them."*

**"He must increase [in prominence], but I must decrease." John 3:30 (AMP)**

(**Baros** is Greek for "burden" and it denotes something heavy.)

### Burdens of the Day

**Matthew 20:12** speaks of the burden of duty to be borne, or a difficult requirement. **Acts 15:28; Revelation 2:24** speak of the burden of one's moral infirmities, while **Galatians 6:2** speaks of carrying one another's burdens.

In **Jeremiah 23:38**, the "burden of the LORD" refers to a prophecy from God. That's why the original Greek word translated as *burden* in **Jeremiah 23:38** is translated as *prophecy* in **Proverbs 30:1** and **Proverbs 31:1**

In Hebrew, **massa**, (from the root word **nasa**,) means "He lifted up." Thus, literally any load is called *massa*. **Exodus 23:5, Numbers 4:15, 24, 27, 2 Kings 5:17; 8:9**

When a prophet develops a burden of the Lord, the root word here, *nasa*, means "*He* lifts up," not "*you*." *Not* your personality, *not* your popularity, *not* your politics, and *not* your gift. God is the One who *can* and *will* raise you up and exalt you. The deeper the burden gets in the life of the prophetic ministry gift or the prophet of the Lord, the more likely it is that they will begin to experience a *nasa*.

**"I said to the arrogant, 'Do not boast;' and to the wicked, 'Do not lift up the horn [of self-glorification].**

Do not lift up your [defiant and aggressive] horn on high, do not speak with a stiff neck.' For not from the east, nor from the west, Nor from the desert comes exaltation. But God is the Judge; He puts down one and lifts up another." Psalms 75:4-7 (AMP)

"Therefore, humble yourselves under the mighty hand of God [set aside self-righteous pride], so that He may exalt you [to a place of honor in His service] at the appropriate time." 1 Peter 5:6 (AMP)

*Chapter 11*

# THE BURDEN OF THE PROPHETIC

- **B**ow continuously (implies submission)
- **U**nderstand your Purpose
- **R**eset others with Revelation
- **D**etermined to see Destiny in Others
- **E**liminates Excuses
- **N**avigates you through the Process of Life

*"A prophet that carries the burden of the Lord will never be (or become) comfortable."*

I believe that every prophet and prophetic ministry gift should be weighed down with the burden of the Lord. There should be something that weighs heavily on you in reference to the things of God. There are so many advances that the devil will try to make towards the prophetic ministry gifts, because he knows that if he can keep the people of God away from the prophetic, they will remain in a cycle of defeat. When a prophet of God develops a burden for the Lord, he or she will not let friends, situations, material things or relationships keep them from declaring the Word of the Lord.

When a prophet of God has the burden of the Lord:

They have a revelation of the **Word** of God
They have a revelation of the **Will** of God
They have a revelation of **Worshipping** God
They have a revelation of the **Ways** of God
They have a revelation of the **Wisdom** of God

The world has seen so much in the context of the "church." We confess that we are Christians, but then our lifestyles contradict that. Now, people don't want anything to do with the church. This is why I'm believing that in this season, God is raising up prophets and prophetic presbytery for the Body of Christ to advance out of defeat, depression, and fear, break strongholds, and emerge victorious from the vice grip of religion. People in this world are hurting, and we need the prophets of God to stand up and prophesy with *boldness, clarity,* and *faith*.

> *Prophets that develop the burden of the Lord will not compromise or settle for anything other than the Word of the Lord, be it for a nation, a region, or the local church.*

**"I will stand at my guard post And station myself on the tower; And I will keep watch to see what He will say to me, And what answer I will give [as His spokesman] when I am reproved. Then the Lord answered me and said, 'Write the vision and engrave it plainly on [clay] tablets so that the one who reads it will run. For the vision is yet for the appointed [future] time. It hurries toward the goal [of fulfillment]; it will not fail. Even though it delays, wait [patiently] for it, because it will certainly come; it will not delay.'" Habakkuk 2:1-3 (AMP)**

Notice in this text how the prophet Habakkuk stated, "I will stand at my post." Every prophet may not have the same post, but as prophets, we all share the same purpose, and that is to *hear from God, remain in a place of holiness, release the Word of the Lord* as the Spirit of God leads us, and **always point people back to Jesus.**

As a young prophet just coming into the prophetic, I was not always led by the Lord. There were times when

*The Burden of the Prophetic*

I spoke what I felt... and missed it miserably. A lot of that had to do with a lack of training. Being inexperienced, I was not willing to admit that at times, I just didn't get it, and didn't know it all. It wasn't until sometime later that I began to get a revelation and understanding of the prophetic gift. My faith was challenged and stretched, but I knew that God was taking me somewhere that I had never been before... and I was ready.

Something began to erupt on the inside of me that I can't really explain. There was a prophetic gift on the horizon. There was a prophetic seed that was beginning to bud, and in order for it to flourish, I knew I had to find a place to "get planted" so that it could grow. I left a very religious organization and crossed over into the charismatic movement. I found a church that flowed in the gifts of the Spirit.

Do I regret it?

*Absolutely not!* I am so glad that God loved me enough not to let me stay in that state! Now, as growing prophets, all of us have encountered this to some degree. We may have thought what we heard was the Lord, when actually, it wasn't. The church is in need of prophets and prophetic people to get wisdom concerning their assignments and gifting. The burden of the Lord will push you into the pursuit of learning and discovering as it related to your prophetic destiny. It took some time for this to occur for me, but when that burden kicked in, I was ready to hear, ready to pray, ready to worship and praise, and ready to learn and prophesy!

I remember years ago like it was yesterday... myself and two of my best friends, young and on fire for God. It didn't matter if no one else wanted to... we made up our minds that *we* would. In Chicago, we have what is known as the Red Line. The train runs north and south, starting at 95th, and Dan Ryan, and goes (I believe) to the Howard stop on the north side of the city. All three of us were fairly new to the prophetic, but I guess in a sense, I was the front runner... kind of like John the Baptist. (You want to talk about a burden?) We used to get up early in the morning, before our work days started, and ride the train from one end to the other at least twice. Before this, I had been the one *hiding* when someone would get on the train and start declaring the Word of the Lord. We would get on the train, and take turns preaching, prophesying or praying at like 5 or 6 in the morning, at least a few times a week. We did this for a while and eventually grabbed others along with us. It was priceless just to get on the trains at that time of the morning and witness the faces of the people as they saw three young (nice-looking, I might add!) young men, preaching about a man called Jesus. There were times when we would literally have people so engaged that they would start crying and couldn't explain what was happening to them... but we knew!

We loved God with our hearts as young men. Were we perfect? Absolutely not! No one on this planet is perfect. But we had a burden for souls and loved seeing people come to know the Lord for the first time. It was priceless! All of us are now happily married, with our own families, and most importantly, we're still on fire for God. I can say this in confidence—our fire for Him has only increased! **(Love you guys both to life, Trenton Teat and Lamont Reid!)**

Let me share with you another amazing story. This one actually involves my unbelievably amazing wife. I met her at her church. At the time she was attending a church on the south side of Chicago. She was the director of the performing arts ministry, as well as the director of outreach and evangelism. She had her hands in several aspects of the ministry. I was so impressed by the focus and love that she had for God, (not to mention that she's gorgeous!) I remember at some point after visiting this church, my best friends and I all eventually joined, one after the next. There was a group of us young people in our early twenties that wanted to impact the world with the Gospel of Reconciliation. We all would meet at a certain location, have prayer, hand out assignments, and go out like the disciples—two by two. I remember that as young adults, we would sacrifice every Saturday night to go out and witness on the streets of south Chicago.

The area we used to hit was on 79th and Cottage Grove, in front of the Happy Liquor Store. We'd meet up there faithfully around 9/9:30 pm, and pray, prophesy, and invite people to church. There was another liquor store adjacent to the Happy Liquor Store, and through prayer and anointing the place and the ground, I am proud to say that they shut down the operation and "got out of Dodge." The Happy Liquor Store was (and still is) a demonic stronghold in that community. Others have attempted to get it moved or shut down and unfortunately, it's still standing.

We saw many miracles during our time of witnessing on the streets of Chicago. If you're not familiar with the south side of Chicago, let me help you. 79th St., which runs east and west, is one of the most crime-infested, gang-infiltrated, prostitution-infested, drug-plagued parts of the city. There's a strong spirit of murder, violence, and poverty in that community, but God is raising up a vessel in the area. He's Pastor John Hannah, who is taking a stand and impacting the community for the Lord.

One Saturday night, we were out witnessing, as we did almost every weekend. I was with my friend, Lamont Reid. A very tall gentleman came out of the store with a brown paper bag balled up in his hand, and truth be told—we prejudged him. Lamont and I stopped him and asked him if he would mind if we prayed for him. He said, "Of course, go right ahead." We took turns praying for him, and when we were both finished, he asked, "Now can I pray for you guys?" We looked at each other and were kind of caught off guard. We said, "Okay, no problem." The man began to pray, and to our amazement, God showed up! I believe that it was because we had a burden to witness without anyone making us do it. All of a sudden, the man squeezed my hand, looked me in the eye, and said, "Young man, you're a prophet!" Then he went on and said, "You want to know how I know? You are holding the hand of a prophet!" Lamont and I were blown away at how the Lord had shown up in a very unexpected way that night. Then he began to prophesy many other things about my life and family, even telling me that I would be getting married soon. "And the one you're going to marry is out here with you tonight!" My knees began to buckle and my heart was pounding in my chest.

Then he began to prophesy to my friend Lamont about being an evangelist. He went on to tell him how he saw his mouth moving a lot, (as to say he's always talking) and all of us who knew Lamont knew that was very true (but in a good way, of course).

I also recall one Saturday night when we were praying for a young man who couldn't have been older than 17 or 18. He was affiliated with one of the gangs in that area, but he was willing to let us minister to him and pray for him. Little did we know, days later, someone would put a hit out on his life. I was coming home one day on the bus, and I noticed there were police cars everywhere. The Holy Spirit said to me, "That was the young man that you guys prayed for." Eventually, I made my way to the scene, and was talking to one of his guys (we had met previously, I believe). He told me that his friend had been shot in the face. Later, I talked to someone who told me that the young man's aunt had moved him out-of-town and that he survived. I firmly believe that it was because of the prayers of the righteous.

In both of these instances, notice how all of us as young adults developed the burden of the Lord. We just didn't talk the talk... we walked the walk!

**"For the creation waits in eager expectation for the children of God to be revealed. For the creation was subjected to frustration, not by its own choice, but by the will of the one who subjected it, in hope that the creation itself will be liberated from its bondage to decay and brought into the freedom and glory of the children of God." Romans 8:19-21 (NIV)**

*"When a prophet of God has the burden of the Lord, they don't function under hidden agendas."*

Unfortunately, today in our local assemblies, we have prophetic gifts who do whatever, or say whatever, and go wherever, and they lack the burden of the Lord. When the prophets of God develop the burden, they may wake up while others are asleep, they may fast while others are eating, they may study the Scriptures with such a hunger for the Word of God, and declare what others may not be willing to say because they aren't graced. In addition to correction, prophets also release direction into the life of believers. The burden of the Lord will cause you to be selective, and not settle for sin or anything that's contrary to His Word.

One of my favorite prophets and kings in the Old Testament is Jehu, who is not often discussed in our worship services. I believe that Jehu had an anointing that we need to see more of in the church today. He had a confrontational, relentless spirit, and he was focused on the assignment at hand. I declare, *"Lord, release the fire, drive and passion of Jehu!"*

"Now Elisha the prophet called one of the sons of the prophets and said to him, 'Gird up your loins (prepare for action), take this flask of oil in your hand and go to Ramoth-gilead. When you arrive there, look for Jehu the son of Jehoshaphat the son of Nimshi, and go in and have him arise from among his brothers, and take him into an inner room. Then take the flask of oil and pour it on his head and say, "Thus says the Lord: 'I have anointed you king over Israel.'" Then open the door and flee and do not delay.' So the young man, the servant of the prophet, went to Ramoth-gilead. When he arrived, the captains of the army were sitting [outside]; and he said, 'I have a message for you, O captain.' Jehu said, 'To which one of us?' And he said, 'For you, O captain.'

So Jehu got up, and they went into the house. And he poured the oil on Jehu's head and said to him, 'Thus says the Lord, the God of Israel: "I have anointed you king over the people of the Lord, over Israel. You shall strike the house of Ahab your master, so that I may avenge the blood of My servants the prophets, and the blood of all the servants of the Lord, [who have died] at the hands of Jezebel. For the entire house of Ahab shall perish, and I will cut off from Ahab every male, both bond and free, in Israel. I will make the house of Ahab like the house of Jeroboam the son of Nebat, and like the house of Baasha the son of Ahijah. And the dogs will eat Jezebel in the territory of Jezreel, and there will be no one to bury her."' Then he opened the door and fled." 2 Kings 9:1-10 (AMP)

The Bible talks of this man called Jehu, who played a vital part in the assassination of Jezebel. He was a king of Israel noted for his furious chariot attacks. His name not only means "Jehovah is he", but also (and I love this part), "a skilled driver, and one who is fast!" This makes me think of the movie *The Fast and the Furious,* with all of the skilled drivers. This is what we need... someone who's going to be swift, and not play with the devil. Someone who knows what they are doing. *God, let this anointing increase on those appointed!* The author of Second Kings goes on to tell us that Jehu entered the city without resistance. He saw Jehoram's mother, Jezebel, watching him with contempt from a palace window.

Jehu commanded the palace eunuchs to throw her from the window. In other words, he was saying, "You don't have to be under her control anymore. You are free, so start acting and living like you are a man or woman of God!"

> *This word is for someone right now, and if you're reading this, God is ministering to you! You must know that God never intended for you to be bound up in religion, inside of a "box." I declare unto you; the time is now to awaken from your place of slumber. Begin to lift your hands, right where you are, and go after God!*

Jezebel was killed, and Jehu drove his chariot over her body. Off the tower she went, and down to the ground she fell. Her servants later came to bury her, only to find that the dogs had eaten all but her hands, feet, and skull.

We need an impartation of the "Jehu Anointing" today in our churches. The Bible declares that Jehu drove "furiously." He was focused on his objective and that was to get Jezebel off of that tower, overthrow her, and throw her down! Jezebel doesn't belong in our worship services. We have had that spirit there too long in a place of power and authority. Let God raise up someone who is not intimidated by religion and tradition, someone willing to "go against the grain!"

We need Jehus in the Body of Christ today! Let's take back our authority in worship, and our authority in the kingdom. If you read the story of Jehu, you'll notice how he even left the door open, as if to say, "This isn't going to take long. I'm not here to waste your time or my time. We are about to *handle this*, and it's not going to take forever." This is the same prophet of God who gathered hundreds of Baal worshippers together and killed them.

> *Lord, I declare that you spark and ignite a flame in the prophets of God like you did in Jehu. Let the Jehus arise in the north, in the south, in the east and in the west!*

When there is a burden from the Lord, you find:

- Unprecedented **service**
- No **squabbles**
- You are **firm** in His promises and in His Word
- You are **steered** by the Holy Spirit
- You have **structure** in your life
- You remain a **student** for life—always learning and growing

We need more prophets today who are overwhelmed with the burden of the Lord. The prophets who lack character in the prophetic also lack in carrying the burden of the Lord as well.

It's amazing how many prophetic gifts in the church are driven by their natural sight rather than by their spirit. As prophets of the Lord, we walk in unfamiliar territory and uncomfortable places, and we walk in realms in the prophetic that the average Christian does not. I can't sit here and tell you that being a prophet of God is going to be easy, and that everyone will welcome you. Jesus Himself was a prophet and we must remember all of what He had to go through to fulfill His destiny. Walking in this office comes with a great price. I know this personally from experience.

There was a season of my life where I was homeless in Chicago, disconnected from my immediate family, and disconnected from the friends that I had grown up with. It was not easy to say, "I must part ways from here, because if I don't, I'll abort my destiny and perhaps the lives of some of those who were connected to me" if I walked away from my assignment. I can recall the times when I cried inside and felt like I was deserted and misunderstood. I felt like I might as well go back out into the world and just live for the devil. As the voices were sounding off in my head and my heart all over the place, the war at some point began for my soul. It was time to make a decision.

Let me take this opportunity to encourage someone right here and right now. You cannot afford to let the enemy infect your mind because when this happens, it affects your life. God has placed something unique in us all. Walking in the office of a prophet or prophetic ministry will not come without accusation, persecution, and misunderstanding, but if God *called you*, He has also *equipped you*. The life of a prophet comes with several prerequisites: isolation, loneliness, misunderstanding, ridicule, abandonment, being disowned and ignored by others, and rejection. Believe me when I say this, you can overcome this wilderness or weary season of your life. The devil is not going to give up, but you have to make up in your mind that you're not going to quit either! Someone of you that may be reading this book now know that God's hand has been on your life since you were a child, and now the time has come to accept the calling of God to the prophetic ministry. Begin to inquire. Attend the prophetic gatherings in your region. I'm not saying every one of them, but be led by the Spirit of God.

You may even be a pastor and the Spirit of God has been dealing with you—you've noticed that you've had an unusual urge to explore deeper in the gifts of the Spirit.

I prophesy, *right now*, that *where you are right now is not where you are going!* The time to expand your spirit man is now. I declare that your church will encounter a breath of fresh air like never before, and that signs and wonders on a whole new level will be manifested.

Chapter 12

# THOROUGHBREDS AND BLACK STALLIONS

A Thoroughbred is a horse breed best known for its use in horseracing. Thoroughbreds are considered purebred and are "hot-blooded." These horses are best known for their agility, speed, and spirit.

I am convinced that as born-again believers, there is a need to train, equip, and prepare those who are longing to function in this capacity. It's what I want to call spending time in the "Prophetic Stables." It's not until we begin to discern the prophetic gift that we will learn. The interesting thing about stables is that they house horses until a set time—when they feel that they are ready to run the race. Like with most things, there is a process to go through to get to that point.

There are people who believe they can become a wonder overnight. When horses are groomed for racing, it requires effort, investment, time, energy, and patience. To produce a winning thoroughbred is costly. I believe that in this hour, God is going to raise up prophetic thoroughbreds, those who are skilled and trained, equipped and balanced in the Word and the things of God. The Samuels are rising... the Obadiahs are rising... and none of their words will fall to the ground without bearing fruit. In our churches, we have evolved into a culture that instantly wants it all. There is a lack of *credibility* because of a lack of *accountability*.

We are now seeing people who want to be prophetic, but they have what I am labeling a "Black Stallion Spirit." It's the mindset that says, "I know it all. I am good. I am okay. Let me be." It's a spirit that refuses to submit, is not easily broken, and is unruly and untamed, with a mind of its own.

One of the most interesting things about Thoroughbred horses is that they don't like for anyone to ride them. They want to steer themselves, move when they want to move, and stay still if they want to. "Black Stallions" are often the ones who are untrained and unlearned. They have a rebellious nature ingrained in their being, so that makes it difficult for others to assist or help guide them.

They're like certain people who, when it comes to the prophetic ministry, are rebels. They go from place to place prophesying and have no covering. You know the ones—they don't think they have to follow protocol, and they think that for some reason, they are above authority and order. For example, you have parking lot prophets, bathroom prophets, and divisive prophets. These are the ones who seek to sow disorder and seeds of distraction and cause a disagreement between the members and leaders. Generally, their facial expressions would indicate that they don't see you or recognize your gifting. But the next thing you know, they will try and pull you to the side and attempt to prophesy to you, even after the pastor or set leader has already done so. Beware of disorderly prophets!

I believe that in this season, God will raise up prophetic voices that will mentor other prophetic gifts. In other words, an authentic mentor, who has your permission to travel through life with you until you reach your prophetic destiny. This is one of the reasons why I really felt so impressed to write this book, to be able to connect with other up-and-coming prophets and prophetic gifts.

One of the most amazing prophets to me was the Prophet Obadiah. The Book of Obadiah is the shortest one in the Old Testament; however, it is impactful and powerful.

**Obadiah** "by the numbers" ...

- **31st** book of the Bible
- **1** chapter
- **21** verses
- **670** words
- **1** command
- **4** questions
- **30** predictions
- **12** verses of prophecy
- **5** verses of fulfilled prophecy
- **7** verses of unfulfilled prophecy
- **3** distinct messages from God

Another interesting fact about the Prophet Obadiah was that he was of the tribe of Issachar.

**"...from Issachar, men who understood the times and knew what Israel should do—200 chiefs, with all their relatives under their command..." 1 Chronicles 12:32 (NIV)**

He was serving as a prophet and governor in the house of Ahab and Jezebel (**1 Kings 18:3-16**). He had developed such a passion for the prophetic and the prophets of God that he eventually risked his own life to save them. The young prophet of God took it upon himself to nurture and care for one hundred prophets. If you look between the lines, Obadiah was not a "broke" prophet. Apparently, he had the means to provide for these prophets that he hid in the caves. He took fifty and hid them in one cave and he took the other fifty and hid them in another cave. During his tenure, he dealt with the people of Edom, the descendants of Esau, who had sold his birthright for a meal. The Edomites were known for their pride, which opens the door to sin. If you notice, both the word "pride" and the word "sin" both have the letter "I" exactly in the middle. Obadiah rose up in his day to deal with something we often struggle with as Christians even today—pride and sin.

Here are several Scriptures that warn us against having a spirit of pride.

**"Who is it you have ridiculed and blasphemed? Against whom have you raised your voice and lifted your eyes in pride? Against the Holy One of Israel!" 2 Kings 19:22 (NIV)**

**"In his pride, the wicked man does not seek him; in all his thoughts there is no room for God." Psalms 10:4 (NIV)**

**"When pride comes, then comes disgrace, but with humility comes wisdom." Proverbs 11:2 (NIV)**

**"Pride goes before destruction, a haughty spirit before a fall." Proverbs 16:18 (NIV)**

**"Pride brings a person low, but the lowly in spirit gain honor." Proverbs 29:23 (NIV)**

**"The eyes of the arrogant will be humbled and human pride brought low; the Lord alone will be exalted in that day." Isaiah 2:11 (NIV)**

**"The pride of your heart has deceived you, you who live in the clefts of the rocks and make your home on the heights, you who say to yourself, 'Who can bring me down to the ground?'" Obadiah 1:3 (NIV)**

"For everything in the world—the lust of the flesh, the lust of the eyes, and the pride of life—comes not from the Father but from the world." 1 John 2:16 (NIV)

Don't become a Gehazi!

"When Elisha the man of God heard that the king of Israel had torn his robes, he sent him this message: 'Why have you torn your robes? Have the man come to me and he will know that there is a prophet in Israel.' So Naaman went with his horses and chariots and stopped at the door of Elisha's house. Elisha sent a messenger to say to him, 'Go, wash yourself seven times in the Jordan, and your flesh will be restored and you will be cleansed.'"

"But Naaman went away angry and said, 'I thought that he would surely come out to me and stand and call on the name of the Lord his God, wave his hand over the spot and cure me of my leprosy. Are not Abana and Pharpar, the rivers of Damascus, better than all the waters of Israel? Couldn't I wash in them and be cleansed?' So he turned and went off in a rage. Naaman's servants went to him and said, 'My father, if the prophet had told you to do some great thing, would you not have done it? How much more, then, when he tells you, 'Wash and be cleansed'!" So he went down and dipped himself in the Jordan seven times, as the man of God had told him, and his flesh was restored and became clean like that of a young boy."

"Then Naaman and all his attendants went back to the man of God. He stood before him and said, 'Now I know that there is no God in all the world except in Israel. So please accept a gift from your servant.' The prophet answered, 'As surely as the Lord lives, whom I serve, I will not accept a thing.' And even though Naaman urged him, he refused. 'If you will not,' said Naaman, 'please let me, your servant, be given as much earth as a pair of mules can carry, for your servant will never again make burnt offerings and sacrifices to any other god but the Lord. But may the Lord forgive your servant for this one thing: When my master enters the temple of Rimmon to bow down and he is leaning on my arm and I have to bow there also—when I bow down in the temple of Rimmon, may the Lord forgive your servant for this.' 'Go in peace,' Elisha said. After Naaman had traveled some distance, Gehazi, the servant of Elisha the man of God, said to himself, 'My master was too easy on Naaman, this Aramean, by not accepting from him what he brought. As surely as the Lord lives, I will run after him and get something from him.'"

"So Gehazi hurried after Naaman. When Naaman saw him running toward him, he got down from the chariot to meet him. 'Is everything alright?' he asked. 'Everything is all right,' Gehazi answered. 'My master sent me to say, "Two young men from the company of the prophets have just come to me from the hill country of Ephraim. Please give them a talent of silver and two sets of clothing."'

'By all means, take two talents,' said Naaman. He urged Gehazi to accept them, and then tied up the two talents of silver in two bags, with two sets of clothing. He gave them to two of his servants, and they carried them ahead of Gehazi. When Gehazi came to the hill, he took the things from the servants and put them away in the house. He sent the men away and they left. When he went in and stood before his master, Elisha asked him, 'Where have you been, Gehazi?'

'Your servant didn't go anywhere,' Gehazi answered. But Elisha said to him, 'Was not my spirit with you when the man got down from his chariot to meet you? Is this the time to take money or to accept clothes—or olive

**groves and vineyards, or flocks and herds, or male and female slaves? Naaman's leprosy will cling to you and to your descendants forever.' Then Gehazi went from Elisha's presence and his skin was leprous—it had become as white as snow." 2 Kings 5:8-27 (NIV)**

Because of the nature of what I'm about to express, I know it's not one of those things that will necessarily make you shout... however, I believe Heaven will shout.

Earlier this year, the spirit of the Lord spoke to me and said, *"I'm about to deal with the 'Gehazis in the area of the prophetic. Many of the prophets in this hour think they're getting away with being in error, but not so! For I am about to judge the prophetic ministry and for those who have responded as Gehazi. I will release a spiritual leprosy over their lives that will cause people to go in the opposite direction from them, for I will begin to take their audience from them. No longer will these people be able to function and flow and navigate, for I am the Lord your God, and I am raising up prophetic order, prophetic balance, structure, and foundation saith the Lord."* (Prophecy)

The prophetic has been misused and abused for too long. In this story, I want you to see how important it is as a prophet or prophetic presbytery to function in this capacity of the prophetic without an ulterior motive. The prophet Elijah prepared Elisha for his prophetic assignment, and the prophet Elisha was in the process of passing on the torch to his protégé, Gehazi. We see in the story that Elisha stated, "I'm good. I'm okay, and we appreciate the offer." I believe that what Elisha was really saying is "I'm not in this for the fame, the game or to make a name for myself. I'm not in this for the accolades. I'm not in this to see my face on someone's flyer, or to build my itinerary. I'm in this because I want to go where 'everybody knows my name.'" (To quote the theme song from *Cheers*).

I believe that it was a heart check moment for Elisha as well as Gehazi. Elisha, the man who moved in at least *thirty-two supernatural miracles* in his tenure, stated, "Keep what you have Naaman. I'm in this to serve God." Naaman (of course) tried his best to bless the prophet. I'm not saying that there is anything wrong with sowing into the life of the prophet; however, as prophets, we can never make it all about the money. I could only imagine what was going through Gehazi's head. "Is this guy Elisha out of his cotton-picking mind? We got a chance to get some nice money here!" Now, what we may have not seen here was that I believe Gehazi might have been "winking his eye" at Naaman, saying, "I know what my mentor is saying, but I will be right back—don't change your mind." If Gehazi had had a cell phone, he would've texted Naaman.

Gehazi did one of the most dangerous things that you can do as a prophet, and that is to allow your heart to be uncovered, or without the Word. One of the things I believe the Lord wanted for me to see was that as a prophet, I need to be cautious and careful not to pull myself away from the principles of God's Word and the principles of the prophetic. Gehazi's name is interpreted as "looking from a low place, such as a valley." Gehazi is almost like the New Testament version of Judas. He was serving close to the man of God, was with him most of the time, and was being trained and mentored by him. Nevertheless, his prophetic perspective and sense of purpose was distorted by the distraction of money.

> *If you're "sometimes up, sometimes down," or you can't go somewhere because they can't give you a $20,000 honorarium, or don't have your favorite water of choice, or won't put you in a 5-star hotel... you have a heart issue.*

Now please hear me. I believe that the ministry that is inviting you should have already made preparations to receive you. My problem is when the money begins to have our hearts, instead of the Holy Spirit. When this occurs, beware of the Gehazi spirit. Gehazi's heart was revealed in this text and the bottom line is, I don't care how you try to fix it up with Greek, Hebrew, Matthew Henry Commentaries, Lexington's, your intellect or your hermeneutics—it is what it is. *The one thing that time will not do is lie. What is in your heart will eventually at some point make its way to the surface.* My question is, was it the position or was it the person?

I believe that Gehazi's downfall had to do with the person his heart revealed that he was. The office, or the title of the prophet, which is the position, stands on the basis of the Word of God. There were several flaws that led to Gehazi's fall.

- He lost his concern for the things and people of God. **(2 Kings 4:27)**
- He failed to serve freely.
- He failed to discern what God was doing.

I often say that when it comes to walking in the office of a prophet, you must master the art of *learning* and *listening*. You can graduate from grammar school, high school and even college, but the one place you can never graduate from is the place of learning in life. If you have backed away from the principle of the prophetic... then perhaps you are nothing but a true profit after all. *Selah*.

Elisha's prophetic perspective was in an elevated place, so he saw that it was good to pass on the gifts from Naaman. I believe we are about to see the rising of the Prophetic Thoroughbreds and the Obadiahs, and they will crack the concrete of greed and deception in the prophetic. This is the kind of prophet that merges with the Word instead of the world. This is why there is a stirring in the prophetic; the purity, passion, and purpose of the prophetic is coming back!

The sad thing here is that this Gehazi spirit, if not checked in the prophetic, can abort or contaminate the up and coming Obadiahs in this hour. Let this be your prayer and declaration: *"Father, do not let me ever move away from your principles of the prophetic. Keep my heart clean so that I can remain focused, and never have it said of me that I became a Gehazi. I declare that prophetic authority is about to increase in the lives of the prophets of God, for the time has come to move in another dimension of power and demonstration."*

I remember years ago, when I was just coming into the prophetic ministry, I used to have a lot of dreams, and didn't often always understand all of them. However, there was one I remember fairly well.

I was on my way to church, and I remember being by myself. At some point, I began to feel as though I was being followed, and to my surprise, as I turned around, there was someone there following me. I began to walk a little faster, and for some strange reason fear had started to infiltrate my mind. I noticed that every time I looked back, it seemed as though the crowd had grown. It kept increasing in size and number, and I got really nervous at this point. I remember changing directions, and I found myself literally running for what I assumed was my life. But I kept hearing these words and looking at their hands. When I began to focus on their hands, I noticed that they were carrying every imaginable weapon you could think of. There were guns, knives, grenades, bazookas, machetes, you name it—they had it. I remember at some point thinking that these people were going to kill me if I didn't find somewhere to hide. I eventually found myself running out into what looked like an open field. I had nowhere else to run or hide. The people started making a lot of noise, saying things like, "We've got you now! Where are you going to go now?" Of course, fear had me to the point where I believe I froze for a moment. I remember praying in my spirit, "God, I need your help! You've got to get me out of this, Lord!" I kid you not—all of a sudden, the ground around me literally began to shake, and I felt the ground around me rise—almost like a small stage. I felt myself being elevated over my adversaries. The people in the audience began to raise their hands, as if they were about to strike, then I heard the Lord say, "Open your mouth, son, and declare Jesus!" I did exactly that, and all of a sudden, the fire of God came out of my mouth, and it began to consume everyone around me. They all were destroyed when the fire hit them. This is just the skinny of the dream I had.

Later that same week, I had what appeared to be almost the same dream, but this time it was a woman with her face covered in a gown, or some type of formal dress or something. I remember going back almost to the exact same place in my last dream and the short version was that this lady chased me to the same place that I had been before and said, "I know who you are, and you're not going to make it—I'm going to destroy you." I was so afraid. I couldn't see her face, but in this dream, it was a little different. I remember that the fear was so strong that I couldn't even speak—my words were like I was mumbling or something. We were at the same place in the field, when all of a sudden, the ground around me began to rise up again. This lady would not reveal her face. I honestly thought I was going to die.

I kept hearing the word "Jesus" in my head, but for some reason, my mouth was disconnected from my mind. I kept on saying "Jesus" in my head, and then I heard the Lord say, "Son, trust me. I got you. Now open your mouth and **declare my name**!" I did just that, and to my surprise, His name rolled off of my lips, and I felt power like I've never experienced before. Then right before my eyes, I witnessed the fire of God as it was released from my mouth and spirit. It hit that woman and she literally began to shake, and eventually exploded right in front of my face. (Remember—all of this occurred within the same week.) Later, I got the interpretation of my being a prophet, and Jezebel sending out her army to destroy me and they couldn't, so the Spirit Himself had come. To God be the glory though, I have received so much clarity and confirmation about who God was raising me up to be... a Prophetic Thoroughbred.

*Chapter 13*

# THE RIGHT PROPHETIC COMPANY

*"When you discover your difference, you'll discover your destiny and when you know your difference, you'll learn your passion."*

*"When place meets timing then purpose will be revealed."*

**"Multitudes, multitudes in the valley of decision! For the day of the Lord is near in the valley of decision." Joel 3:14 (NIV)**

The Body of Christ is full of believers who are frustrated, misunderstood and unsatisfied, and who feel as though they are out of place. For this very reason, I need you to declare this out loud with me:

*"I will walk in everything God has for me. I will have everything that God has designed for me. If this means that I have to leave certain people, then so be it. If it means I have to relocate, then so be it. My life will increase in this season. I will connect with the right people, and it will not tarry. Lord, I am ready now to be stretched in every area of my life. I'm mounting up right now!"*

I don't know about you, but I'm so glad that I'm at a point in my life where I'm getting more than a word somebody just studied or a word based on their degrees. I want dimensions and degrees in the Spirit. I need an impartation!

It's important to be in the right place at the right time, because when this happens, *place* will meet *purpose*. The Body of Christ is full of believers who are not really connecting where they currently are. This doesn't make that ministry a bad place; however, for you, the right place is very important, because when you find it, your purpose will be awakened and discovered. Nothing is more frustrating than wanting to grow and flow in the things of God as it relates to your destiny; but because of where you are, you have become stuck or stagnant! God has a purpose for us all, but it can only come to fruition if you're in the right place at the right time. Then... and only then... will the right place meet with purpose! So many people get trapped in the valley of indecision and can't function because of so many things going on in their lives and their world. People are indecisive, uncertain, and unstable, because they're not in congruence with the plan of God concerning their lives. In other words, many believers are not flowing parallel with the purpose of God. I believe many Christians are asking this question, "How will I ever arrive at the place I'm supposed to be in?" Do you not know you can be working for a company at the right time when a merger happens, and your income can change in a moment?

I know that we place a lot of emphasis on *time*, but for a moment, I want to focus on *place*. The fact is, you can't always be with everybody, doing what *they're* doing, because it may not be what God has called *you* to do.

> *You are not an "accident waiting to happen." You are a "purpose that's about to be revealed!"*

The nature of man is to want to feel as though he is a part of something that's greater than himself, and there is **nothing wrong with that**. The problem comes when, as believers, we settle for less than what God has in mind for us. What God has for you, He has designed and purposed for no one else but you! You have been born a child of God, and this is evidence that your purpose is necessary.

I want to stir something up in you, child of God, that will cause you to move from *potential energy* which can often imply dormancy, to a place where you are *kinetic*, where energy is *in motion*! In other words, where you are now walking in your prophetic destiny! Now, you're not second-guessing God... you aren't *wondering* if this is God... you *know* this is God! He has spoken into in your spirit!

**"'For I know the plans I have for you,' declares the Lord, 'plans to prosper you and not to harm you, plans to give you hope and a future.'" Jeremiah 29:11 (NIV)**

**"When the Lord was about to take Elijah up to heaven in a whirlwind, Elijah and Elisha were on their way from Gilgal. Elijah said to Elisha, 'Stay here; the Lord has sent me to Bethel.' But Elisha said, 'As surely as the Lord lives and as you live, I will not leave you.' So they went down to Bethel. The company of the prophets at Bethel came out to Elisha and asked, 'Do you know that the Lord is going to take your master from you today?'**

**'Yes, I know,' Elisha replied, 'so be quiet.'**

**When they had crossed, Elijah said to Elisha, 'Tell me, what can I do for you before I am taken from you?'**

**'Let me inherit a double portion of your spirit,' Elisha replied.**

**'You have asked a difficult thing,' Elijah said, 'yet if you see me when I am taken from you, it will be yours—otherwise, it will not.'**

**As they were walking along and talking together, suddenly a chariot of fire and horses of fire appeared and**

**separated the two of them, and Elijah went up to heaven in a whirlwind. Elisha saw this and cried out, 'My father! My father! The chariots and horsemen of Israel!' And Elisha saw him no more. Then he took hold of his garment and tore it in two. Elisha then picked up Elijah's cloak that had fallen from him and went back and stood on the bank of the Jordan. He took the cloak that had fallen from Elijah and struck the water with it. 'Where now is the Lord, the God of Elijah?' he asked. When he struck the water, it divided to the right and to the left, and he crossed over. The company of the prophets from Jericho, who were watching, said, 'The spirit of Elijah is resting on Elisha.' And they went to meet him and bowed to the ground before him. 'Look,' they said, 'we your servants have fifty able men. Let them go and look for your master. Perhaps the Spirit of the Lord has picked him up and set him down on some mountain or in some valley.'" 2 Kings 2:1-2, 9-15 (NIV)**

I believe that in this season of your life, God will connect you to a Simeon and a Levi. The Bible states they were instruments of cruelty. They showed no mercy on the enemy and they made sure the job was done. They were part of the crew that went after Adoni-Bezek in the first chapter of the Book of **Judges.** When they caught up with him, they cut off his thumbs and great toes, as he had done to over seventy other kings during his reign. If you know anything about your thumb, you know it is designed to help you grip things. In this case, it implies *establishing order*. The great toes help you with your balance, and without them you'd be completely off-track. This is why I believe this story is prophetic in nature. This is the season where I declare that the Adoni-Bezek's in your life are about to be dealt with. That thing that tried to cripple you, stop you or destroy you will lose its power.

Notice how the Prophet Elijah responds to Elisha: "If you see when I'm taken away, then so will it be unto you a double portion." The implication here is not only the *time* but the *place*. Also, let me bring your attention to the text in **2 Kings 2:10** when Elijah says, "If you see me so shall it be, otherwise it will not."

There is a contingency clause here. You're either going to *get it*... or you're *not*. It's either going to *happen*... or it's *not*. If you'll also notice as they walk together in **2 Kings 2:11**, there was *fellowship*, emphasizing that when you connect with the right prophetic company, there will be fellowship; there was *communication*, and finally, *separation*. Part of the process of coming into your right place will require separation on one end. It is so important to be in the right prophetic company. You don't have time to waste, and you have things to do for the Kingdom.

Here's another thought to consider... every time the prophet Elijah spoke to Elisha, he would use the phrase "And the Lord said." What I'm I getting at, you may ask?

When you're in the right place and in the right prophetic company, the Lord will speak. When you're under the right covering, the Lord will speak to you. Some of you know this firsthand—you have been in some places before where there wasn't much confirmation and revelation. When you're in the right place, you may *see* that you are a man or woman of God, but you *hear* the voice of the Lord for your life and situations.

**"Although the Lord gives you the bread of adversity and the water of affliction, your teachers will be hidden no more; with your own eyes, you will see them. Whether you turn to the right or to the left, your ears will hear a voice behind you, saying, 'This is the way; walk in it.'" Isaiah 30:20-21 (NIV)**

**Prophetic Passages of Scripture:**

"We have also a more sure word of prophecy; where unto ye do well that ye take heed, as unto a light that shineth in a dark place, until the day dawn, and the day star arise in your hearts: Knowing this first, that no prophecy of the scripture is of any private interpretation. For the prophecy came not in old time by the will of man: but holy men of God spake as they were moved by the Holy Ghost." 2 Peter 1:19-21 (KJV)

"But this is that which was spoken by the prophet Joel; And it shall come to pass in the last days, saith God, I will pour out of my Spirit upon all flesh: and your sons and your daughters shall prophesy, and your young men shall see visions, and your old men shall dream dreams: And on my servants and on my hand-maidens I will pour out in those days of my Spirit; and they shall prophesy:" Acts 2:16-18 (KJV)

"Surely the Lord God will do nothing, but he revealeth his secret unto his servants the prophets." Amos 3:7 (KJV)

"But there were false prophets also among the people, even as there shall be false teachers among you, who privily shall bring in damnable heresies, even denying the Lord that bought them, and bring upon themselves swift destruction. And many shall follow their pernicious ways; by reason of whom the way of truth shall be evil spoken of." 2 Peter 2:1-2 (KJV)

"Now concerning spiritual gifts, brethren, I would not have you ignorant. Ye know that ye were Gentiles, carried away unto these dumb idols, even as ye were led. Wherefore I give you to understand, that no man speaking by the Spirit of God calleth Jesus accursed: and that no man can say that Jesus is the Lord, but by the Holy Ghost. Now there are diversities of gifts, but the same Spirit. And there are differences of administrations, but the same Lord. And there are diversities of operations, but it is the same God which worketh all in all. But the manifestation of the Spirit is given to every man to profit withal. For to one is given by the Spirit the word of wisdom; to another the word of knowledge by the same Spirit; To another faith by the same Spirit; to another the gifts of healing by the same Spirit; To another the working of miracles; to another prophecy; to another discerning of spirits; to another diverse kinds of tongues; to another the interpretation of tongues: But all these worketh that one and the self same Spirit, dividing to every man severally as he will." 1 Corinthians 12:1-11 (KJV)

"And Judas and Silas, being prophets also themselves, exhorted the brethren with many words, and confirmed them." Acts 15:32 (KJV)

"Having then gifts differing according to the grace that is given to us, whether prophecy, let us prophesy according to the proportion of faith..." Romans 12:6 (KJV)

"Though I speak with the tongues of men and of angels, and have not charity, I am become as sounding brass, or a tinkling cymbal. And though I have the gift of prophecy, and understand all mysteries, and all knowledge; and though I have all faith, so that I could remove mountains, and have not charity, I am nothing." 1 Corinthians 13:1-2 (KJV)

"Follow after charity, and desire spiritual gifts, but rather that ye may prophesy. Let the prophets speak two or three and let the other judge. If anything be revealed to another that sitteth by, let the first hold his peace. For ye may all prophesy one by one, that all may learn, and all may be comforted. And the spirits of the prophets are subject to the prophets. For God is not the author of confusion, but of peace, as in all churches of the saints. Let all things be done decently and in order." 1 Corinthians 14:1, 29-33, 40 (KJV)

"And are built upon the foundation of the apostles and prophets, Jesus Christ himself being the chief corner stone... " Ephesians 2:20 (KJV)

"And he gave some, apostles; and some, prophets; and some, evangelists; and some, pastors and teachers; For the perfecting of the saints, for the work of the ministry, for the edifying of the body of Christ: Till we all come in the unity of the faith, and of the knowledge of the Son of God, unto a perfect man, unto the measure of the stature of the fullness of Christ..." Ephesians 4:11-13 (KJV)

"Quench not the Spirit. Despise not prophesying. Prove all things; hold fast that which is good." 1 Thessalonians 5:19-21 (KJV)

"Neglect not the gift that is in thee, which was given thee by prophecy, with the laying on of the hands of the presbytery. Meditate upon these things; give thyself wholly to them; that thy profiting may appear to all." 1 Timothy 4:14-15 (KJV)

"Beloved, believe not every spirit, but try the spirits whether they are of God: because many false prophets are gone out into the world." 1 John 4:1 (KJV)

"And I fell at his feet to worship him. And he said unto me, See thou do it not: I am thy fellow servant, and of thy brethren that have the testimony of Jesus: worship God: for the testimony of Jesus is the spirit of prophecy." Revelation 19:10 (KJV)

"But he that prophesieth speaketh unto men to edification, and exhortation, and comfort. Wherefore, brethren, covet to prophesy, and forbid not to speak with tongues." 1 Corinthians 14:3, 39 (KJV)

"We have also a more sure word of prophecy; whereunto ye do well that ye take heed, as unto a light that shineth in a dark place, until the day dawn, and the day star arise in your hearts: Knowing this first, that no prophecy of the scripture is of any private interpretation. For the prophecy came not in old time by the will of man: but holy men of God spake as they were moved by the Holy Ghost." 2 Peter 1:19-21 (KJV)

"Where there is no revelation, the people cast off restraint; But happy is he who keeps the law." Proverbs 29:18 (NKJV)

"God, who at various times and in various ways spoke in time past to the fathers by the prophets," Hebrews 1:1 (NKJV)

"And it shall come to pass afterward, that I will pour out my spirit upon all flesh; and your sons and your daughters shall prophesy, your old men shall dream dreams, your young men shall see visions:" Joel 2:28 (KJV)

# CONCLUSION

We have seen so much that has occurred in the prophetic ministry, but I believe that we are in such an hour where there's a real need for truth and balance. When you look at the state of the church today, it has become a business... and God is left out of it. The prophetic gift has been so diluted and tainted with sin, perversion, and deceit, just to name a few. However, there is a surge of sacrifice going throughout the land. A sacrifice for holiness and doing this thing, the right way.

I have been so stirred in my spirit because I know that the Gads and Obadiahs are being unleashed in the church. That foundation of the prophetic that has been cracked is now being sealed up by prophets and prophetic gifts that desire more than just performance, but to see purpose fulfilled in the Body of Christ. Long live the true nature of the prophetic! The Rising of the Thoroughbreds has begun!

# PROPHETIC CHARGES AND DECREES

I prophesy and declare that your days of being on the ground floor are over, and you're getting ready to take off. It's your Mounting Up Moment! Don't miss it! I declare that things that were stagnant, stuck, restricted, confined, and blocked are about to be released! I prophesy that this will be the season that you arise and take no prisoners. I declare that the backing of heaven is about to connect with you and set you up for life.

I prophesy that the wells of the prophetic will began to stir like never before, and the rivers of wealth will be released over you and your gift. I prophesy that God is about to silence the critics in your life as He releases the unprecedented, the unexpected, the unexplainable, and the undeniable. I declare over you a season of clarity and confirmation, insight, and illumination.

I prophesy that God is throwing your name in the wind and putting your name on the mouths of men.

I prophesy that your gift is about to be exposed and revealed to the world. I decree and declare that there is a bulk-breaking season that's headed your way.

I prophesy that there is a Quantum Grace that's about to be released over your life, and you will increase in measure, amount and quantity on the left and on the right.

I decree and declare that despite where you are, you have a due date scheduled and where you are right now is not where you are going.

I decree and declare that God has expansion, extension, and legacy on His mind for you and your family.

I decree and declare that this next year will be the best of your life, ministry, business, relationships, and marriage.

I prophesy that God is about to set you up for life.

I declare that your days of settling for systems and cycles are over, and that God is now positioning you to soar into a supernatural lifestyle on a regular basis.

I declare that which was impossible before is about to become possible, in Jesus' name.

I declare that your gifting will be used by God to shift and change the world as we know it.

I prophesy that in this season, as you begin to mount up and soar, that your enemies will be revealed and will destroy themselves.

I prophesy that the creative ideas on the inside of you are about to be awoken, activated, and stirred, and that they will cause you to come into your wealthy place in God, and your children's children will be blessed as a result, and the world will see the wealth addition of you.

I decree and declare your season of being down on the floor of life is over. You are about to get up stronger and better than ever before.

I decree and declare that this is your Mounting Up Moment for your prophetic destiny.

Let me release this word over someone right now! Some of you may have had a rough year that may have broken you to the point where you didn't think you were going to make it. But, as the prophet Ezekiel declared over the valley of dry bones, I declare over your life a Divine Reset! I declare that your bones, both natural and spiritual, are about to come back together again, and you will stand stronger than you ever have before; you will overtake, you will recover all, for I, the Lord, am releasing a fresh wind over your lives in this new year! Get ready to breathe again, to prophesy again, to worship, and praise again. I declare that the bones in the church are reviving and will worship again! The four winds of release are blowing even now, and in the wind, will be for you and your house, a Divine Reset!

I prophesy that in 2018, God is about to set many of you back to Manufactured Status! The head and not the tail, above and not beneath. The life that you were created to live is about to manifest and the very people that have been in your life to assassinate or destroy you are about to be dealt with! Some of you couldn't grow because of the weeds among you, but I declare, says the Lord, my hand is moving swiftly and mightily on your behalf, for many things in the natural and spiritual are about to be cut down! For I am the God of recompense!

Supernatural occurrences will become the norm and divine visitations will greatly increase in 2018. For many of you, during the 2:00 am hour, I will begin to visit you like never before, so get ready my sons and daughters, I am releasing my inferno infusion! "For there is much to do, my people," says the Lord, and that time has come! Many of you will become innovators and creators in 2018. You had to go through the fire and flood, and "Now," says the Lord, "am I about to release the geysers of my Glory, for the days of Mounting Up have come. For did I not declare, that which was shall be? I am bringing my sons and daughters into a season of soaring and overcoming." For many of you, know that 2018 will be a year of mounting up and relocating. Many doors of opportunity are opening; do not fret, it's been fixed!

I wanted to release what has been in my spirit since the inception of this last quarter. I heard the Lord say, "Tell my people to reposition, for the time has come to mount up!" There is about to be a supernatural mounting moment for many of you, for even in this last quarter will I release an unexplainable, unexpected, and undeniable grace over your life. What I'm releasing in this last quarter is a "Quantum Grace," over things you could not do, and places you could not go. Know that the time has come for many of you to get up off the floor of life and defeat and rise into the wealth I have ordained for you, for "I will begin to increase your volume, your quantity, your measure and your amount," says the Lord, "Even as I did for my Son Jesus, to whom I gave the Spirit without measure, so shall it be unto you."

I know for many of you this year has been difficult, even rough, but know that my grace is sufficient. For the many of you who have been impacted by worry, which is the design of the enemy to keep you in default, as you continue to worship me, worry will exit. Did I not declare that I came that you might have life and that more abundantly? Do not put a period where I have place a comma! Yes! Live by my design," says the Lord. "For I am overturning and overthrowing the enemy's plans concerning you and your house, and that which is rightfully yours will be released with compounded interest. For as I have favored my servant Cornelius' house, so shall I favor yours. For many of you even in this last month, many things will begin to break. I love you too much to leave you in depression. I love you too much to leave you in lack. I love you too much to leave you in fear. For this cause, I am releasing "The Breaking."

For even I hear the Lord saying, "I have called several of you to be 'Lack Assassinators.' There is a bulk anointing that's about to hit your life." As it hit the Apostle Peter's boat and he had to call for assistance, I declare that you're about to enter into a season where you have to call for help! For I keep hearing even louder in my spirit, "Prepare for The Breaking, prepare for The Breaking!" For even in several of you, ideas will begin to break out of you. "Business plans, miracles, financial freedom, and a life that you never thought you could have," says the Lord, and I even saw in the spirit, FedEx trucks arriving randomly at the homes of many believers in the days to come like never before!

For many of you are about to literally live the Scripture that declares, "Out of your belly shall flow rivers, for many of them have begun to stir up and even rise, rivers of prosperity, rivers of creativity, rivers of wealth," says the Lord, for the year is not over yet!

I declare a **Shabar** over your life! *Shabar*, the Hebrew word for *breaking*, means "to smash into pieces, destroy, fractured, shatter; a tearing down."

*I declare a Shabar in your* **finances**
*I declare a Shabar in your* **health**
*I declare a Shabar in your* **mind**
*I declare a Shabar in your* **marriage**
*I declare a Shabar in your* **job and business**
*I declare a Shabar in your* **ministry pastor**
*I declare a Shabar in your* **house**
*I declare a Shabar in your* **emotions**

I decree and declare that you have been chosen to be a forerunner for finances! 2018 will be a year of Supernatural Mounting! (Prophecy) **Mount Up**!

# A PRAYER OVER THE PROPHETS AND THE PROPHETIC MINISTRY GIFTS

*Lord, cover us with the blanket of humility, wisdom, balance, compassion, grace, and authority. May we be a reflection of Your love and sacrifice. May we demonstrate truth and justice. May we always have a revelation that it's not about self, but service. May our hearts beat after You as a deer pants after the water, and may we always be drawn to the heart of worship. Lord, help us not to smite the prophetic rock as Moses did, but speak when You speak, and just listen when You say listen. Cause our ears to be forever connected to Your mouth. God, help us not to get trapped in making a name, the fame, and the game in prophetic ministry. Keep our eyes focused, and centered on You, so that we won't be distracted by the world, but stand steadfast on the Word of God. May the river of the prophetic flow like a force from Heaven out of our mouths, and our tongues be dipped in fire, and may the dead in spirit be released and activated as we prophesy over them the Word of the Lord. Lord, I declare that the prophets of now will be free, fluent, and flowing in the liberty of the Holy Spirit. I declare that the prophets will be RESET TO RELEASE! In Jesus' name!*

*Thoroughbreds, I charge you to **prophesy**, **decree,** and **declare the Word of Lord!***

*Appendix*

# REFERENCES TO PROPHECY IN THE SCRIPTURES

"Now the rest of the acts of Solomon, first and last, are they not written in the book of Nathan the prophet, and in the prophecy of Ahijah the Shilonite, and in the visions of Iddo the seer against Jeroboam the son of Nebat?" 2 Chronicles 9:29 (KJV)

"And when Asa heard these words, and the prophecy of Oded the prophet, he took courage, and put away the abominable idols out of all the land of Judah and Benjamin, and out of the cities which he had taken from mount Ephraim, and renewed the altar of the Lord, that was before the porch of the Lord." 2 Chronicles 15:8 (KJV)

"And, lo, I perceived that God had not sent him; but that he pronounced this prophecy against me: for Tobiah and Sanballat had hired him." Nehemiah 6:12 (KJV)

"The words of Agur the son of Jakeh, even the prophecy: the man spake unto Ithiel, even unto Ithiel and Ucal..." Proverbs 30:1 (KJV)

"The words of king Lemuel, the prophecy that his mother taught him." Proverbs 31:1 (KJV)

"Seventy weeks are determined upon thy people and upon thy holy city, to finish the transgression, and to make an end of sins, and to make reconciliation for iniquity, and to bring in everlasting righteousness, and to seal up the vision and prophecy, and to anoint the most Holy." Daniel 9:24 (KJV)

"And in them is fulfilled the prophecy of Esaias, which saith, by hearing ye shall hear, and shall not understand; and seeing ye shall see, and shall not perceive..." Matthew 13:14 (KJV)

"Having then gifts differing according to the grace that is given to us, whether prophecy, let us prophesy according to the proportion of faith..." Romans 12:6 (KJV)

"To another the working of miracles; to another prophecy; to another discerning of spirits; to another diverse kinds of tongues; to another the interpretation of tongues..." 1 Corinthians 12:10 (KJV)

"And though I have the gift of prophecy, and understand all mysteries, and all knowledge; and though I have all faith, so that I could remove mountains, and have not charity, I am nothing." 1 Corinthians 13:2 (KJV)

"Neglect not the gift that is in thee, which was given thee by prophecy, with the laying on of the hands of the presbytery." 1 Timothy 4:14 (KJV)

"We have also a more sure word of prophecy; whereunto ye do well that ye take heed, as unto a light that shineth in a dark place, until the day dawn, and the day star arise in your hearts..." 2 Peter 1:19 (KJV)

"Knowing this first, that no prophecy of the scripture is of any private interpretation." 2 Peter 1:20 (KJV)

"For the prophecy came not in old time by the will of man: but holy men of God spake as they were moved by the Holy Ghost." 2 Peter 1:21 (KJV)

"Blessed is he that readeth, and they that hear the words of this prophecy, and keep those things which are written therein: for the time is at hand." Revelation 1:3 (KJV)

"These have power to shut heaven, that it rain not in the days of their prophecy: and have power over waters to turn them to blood, and to smite the earth with all plagues, as often as they will." Revelation 11:6 (KJV)

"And I fell at his feet to worship him. And he said unto me, see thou do it not: I am thy fellow servant, and of thy brethren that have the testimony of Jesus: worship God: for the testimony of Jesus is the spirit of prophecy." Revelation 19:10 (KJV)

"Behold, I come quickly: blessed is he that keepeth the sayings of the prophecy of this book." Revelation 22:7 (KJV)

"And he saith unto me, Seal not the sayings of the prophecy of this book: for the time is at hand." Revelation 22:10 (KJV)

"For I testify unto every man that heareth the words of the prophecy of this book, if any man shall add unto these things, God shall add unto him the plagues that are written in this book..." Revelation 22:18 (KJV)

"And if any man shall take away from the words of the book of this prophecy, God shall take away his part out of the book of life, and out of the holy city, and from the things which are written in this book." Revelation 22:19 (KJV)

"And we beseech you, brethren, to know them which labor among you, and are over you in the Lord, and admonish you..." I Thessalonians 5:12 (KJV)

# ABOUT THE AUTHOR

*"Many call him "The Mail Man" because of his on point prophetic delivery of the Word of God; to others he's an anointed vessel with a 'right now' word for a prepared people..."*

Dr. D. John Coleman is declaring the Word of the Lord during this time; a time which he has labeled "the changing of the guards." He was called by God at the age of 17 and was licensed and ordained at the age of 19 under the Pentecostal Assemblies of the World. (P.A.W.) Dr. John has an AA Degree in Business Management from Phillips College, a Bachelor of Arts in Ministry with an Emphasis on Biblical Studies, a Master of Arts in Christian Education, and a Doctor of Philosophy in Ministry from Midwest Christian College & Seminary.

Dr. John has a mandate to bring a realization to the Body of Christ that it is God's desire for His people to establish a relationship with Him instead of a "religion-ship." He is playing a pivotal part in reaching this generation and equipping them to activate the gifts within them. A cloud of testimonies including financial and healing miracles have manifested as a result of his ministry.

He has traveled and preached locally, nationally, and internationally yet he is committed to his family and church, Kingdom Church Int'l. North and South, a non-denominational, charismatic assembly in which he and his wife are both founders and pastors in the south suburbs of Chicago as well as the inner city. Their vision for both of these locations is to empower God's people for Kingdom living and Kingdom advancement on the earth.

He has authored several other books including, *Power Points to Prosperous Living*, *Chambers of Chenaniah-12 Foundational Truths to Praise & Worship*, *Spiritual Reflections-52 Tips to Prevent Prophetic Slips* and most recently, *Worship Wisdom 424-Reset My Worship.*

Dr. John and his wife, Kisia, live in the south suburbs of Chicago, and are the proud parents of five children; two boys and three girls, including two orphaned nieces and a nephew: Christian, Kennedy, Ca'Koia, Rain, and Jream (**J**esus **R**ules **E**verything **A**round **M**e).

# CONTACT THE AUTHOR

Subscribe to our YouTube @ D. John Coleman Ministries
Facebook @ Deland John Coleman or Prophet D. John Coleman
Twitter @Delandjcoleman
Instagram @ Chenaniahsound

For bookings, contact info@trykci.org.

# TESTIMONIALS

*We give praises to our Almighty God, for He has richly blessed us through Prophet Deland John Coleman, who has truly been a blessing in my personal life and my ministry. His teachings have richly impacted and empowered my life. He is indeed a prophet called by God to educate, equip, and empower God's people.*

**~Prophetess Shirley Hagan**

*Thank you so much, Brother, for what you do for the Kingdom of God! I have been listening to your broadcast, and today, I received the word you gave, and I had a supernatural breakthrough this afternoon. Bless you, Sir, and may the Lord continue to give you favor.*

**~Angelica Santos**

*We have just finished our month-long course, and I thank GOD for Prophet Coleman. This class has given me clarity regarding my call. I have gained so much understanding of the prophetic. If you have any questions about the prophetic, then this class is for you. Thank you, Prophet, for your time, your wisdom, and your mentorship. I pray continued blessings for you and your family.*

**~Pamela Joy Mack,**
**Obadiah Prophetic Mentorship Class**

*I want to take this opportunity to honor a true man of God, who is one of God's true servants. Prophet John is a true voice of God in this hour. A true shepherd for God's children and a true representative of God's Word* and His Kingdom. He has been a mentor to me and many others. May God continue to bless you and keep you and make His face shine upon you. Love you, Prophet John and Pastor Kisia Fells Coleman.

**~Prophetess Jacqueline Gaffney**

On July 16th, our lives were greatly marked by this incredible man of God. He reminded us of who we are, and who God created us to be. There are so many times in life when we forget, or fail to see, what God sees in us. But when God has a plan, He will interrupt routine for destiny. Thank you, Prophet John Coleman.

**~Tony and Joesfina Mendez**

What an awesome experience last evening, spending time with like-minded believers in the presence of the Lord! There certainly is no better place to be, for sure! Prophet D. John Coleman is a GREAT man of God, inspired teacher, and leader in prophetic ministry. I would recommend this instructional class to everyone who has a desire to discover and uncover their spiritual gifts! May our Father in Heaven continue to bless us abundantly, one and all.

**~Diane Shields, Prophetic Boot Camp 101**

I enjoyed the online Prophetic Boot Camp tonight. It was very insightful and clarified many of the misconceptions that I had about the prophetic. Thanks for teaching this course with simplicity, because I was truly able to get an understanding. I highly recommend this class to every believer, so that we can truly bring balance to the prophetic in our churches. Thanks Prophet Coleman for being used by God.

**~Adrienne Adderley, Prophetic Boot Camp 101**

*Prophetic Boot Camp 101... AMAZING!!! So much information in such a short amount of time... So thankful for this teaching! Everyone should take this!*

### ~April Warwick Morris, Prophetic Boot Camp 101

This has been one of the greatest inspirations in my life! The Lord has truly used His servant to confirm some things for me. I have known for a long time that I am called to the prophetic ministry. I would often dream and experience open visions. These dreams would often startle me or leave me feeling perplexed. I would awaken and my husband would interpret them as I began to share them with him.

Intercession was another area where I would experience the Lord dealing with me. I would actually sometimes feel like I was in a physical fight and couldn't understand the exhaustion. I had no understanding of what I was dealing with, because of this I ran from the call. I literally stopped praying for a long time, because I didn't want to deal with it any more.

When Prophet Coleman mentioned tonight that with this office comes principalities and powers, I knew that's just what I was dealing with. I didn't understand it years ago because I didn't feel I had anyone that I could confide in, and that would understand me. I often thought others would just think I was being strange or just crazy. So, I never was at liberty to talk about it.

I'm so grateful that I stumbled upon this man of God and his wife. Thank you again Prophetess Kisia Coleman for connecting me to the call tonight. You are a GEM!!! I am forever grateful for this opportunity to be a part of the Obadiah Prophetic Mentorship Movement! Prophet D. John Coleman, you are truly a man of God. When I first heard you last Thursday morning, I was literally in tears! God's continued blessings upon you and your family! Shalom.

**~Gwendolyn L. Mason-Demby,
Obadiah Prophetic Mentorship Class**

On Sunday, October 2, 2016, I was invited by my sister in Christ, Camilla Martin, to join her at Kingdom Grace Fellowship Church, where Overseer Renea E. Collins is the Senior Pastor. She invited me to their 'Prophetic Encounter Fall Revival' Of course, the day before and the morning of, everything that could happen to prevent me from attending did happen, and I decided not to go. I got back into bed, and then Camilla called me and said, 'God said you need to be there, and I'll wait for you to get ready,' so I did. It was at the revival where I was in the presence of Dr. Coleman, and I intensely listened and received every word of prophecy that was spoken that day. Below is my testimony from my Facebook page this morning and I know my good fortune is a result of me receiving the prophetic word Dr. Coleman spoke of businesses being started in the next 12 months. Additionally, this is only one of the many prophetic words spoken in and over my life that day; I want you all to know that from October 2-December 31 of this year, much of what Dr. Coleman prophesied that day has already manifested in my life. HALLELUJAH!

**~Nichelle Finch**

We so much thank God for Pastors John and Kisia. Not only are they awesome pastors, prophets, and apostles to the nations, but also, they both are great teachers of the Word, and life coaches who encourage you, challenge you and follow you through. It's been just over a year since we started joining their Periscope. The very first teaching that we received was 'SSI: Spirit of Saul

Interference.' I remember that the teaching was so much on point that I quickly grabbed a pen and began taking notes. The teaching and the revelation were so true. Since then, we look forward to, and have been enjoying, their Periscope. They help set the course of my day, and give me the Holy Ghost boost if I am blessed to be able to watch in the early morning. I thank God and praise God for your ever-increasing love and passion for the Lord, for the Word, and for the Body of Christ and people, Pastors John and Kisia! Much love and respect from Tokyo!

**~Setsuko Omoruyi**

I was blessed tremendously by Prophet Coleman. In a very hard time, he released a very timely prophetic word. It was extremely encouraging. I'm thankful for authentic prophetic ministries like this one in our generation.

**~Pastor Chazdon Strickland**

I began to follow Prophet John on Periscope last year, when I noticed that he was a prophet who flowed fluidly, with the Biblical knowledge to go with it. I pray continually for relevant teaching, and that is what he provides. More recently, I had the pleasure of glorifying God with him and his beautiful wife, Kisia Fells Coleman (also a powerhouse for the Lord) when they ministered in Oakland, CA. What a powerfully anointed time of fellowship. The Glory of God definitely had a place to rest that night! I cannot put everything into words that I have received since linking up with this man of God, but I will say this: I have a renewed sense of awe for what God is doing in those who are willing to obey and be His Word. I have learned a great deal about the prophetic and how it fits into the design of God. I also attended prophetic boot camp with Prophet John, and I received guidance and teaching that has really helped me in my ministry. I have seen the uniqueness of a prophet who is not a copycat, but has his own style uniquely created in the throne room ("God-morning!"). I appreciate prophets who give others credit for the Word that God sends through them and doesn't plagiarize like so many do. I see him as someone who is on a prophetic wavelength with the sound of GOD. Wherever that wavelength travels, Prophet John is on it. Thank you, Prophet John.

**~Darnella Melancon**

'Dedicated servant to God's people.' 'Prophet with power, anointing, compassion, and passion.' 'Apostolic arrow.' 'Genuine leader with the heart of a father.' 'Leader of leaders.' These are just few of the words that come to mind when I think of Prophet John, and I feel the same about his wife ('Genuine powerful doer.' 'Faith igniter.') I love these two people right here sincerely. It's been a little over a year now since I was introduced to their ministry through Periscope. I remember that I had just downloaded the app, and had started following people like Apostle Eckhardt, whom I had heard about but never had seen minister. I remember it was a Thursday, and I received a notification about Prophet John being on. I was sitting in my bed studying the Word, and just spending time journaling in silence with the Father, so I thought, 'Okay I'll check him out while I'm sitting here in silence.' Little did I know my whole world was about to be transformed. I watched as he ministered and towards the end he began to prophesy, calling people out. As he did that, I was listening and looking at a Scripture; then I heard the Spirit of the LORD say, 'Look up! I have a word for you.' By that time, Prophet John had called my name, and began to give me the WORD of the LORD. He spoke so many things prophetically that night, things only the SPIRIT of GOD could reveal, one being a passion dear to me that I had been dragging my feet on for various reasons, and one being the finishing of my first book (God had given me 7 book titles at the time.) I can go on and on about how he and his wife literally helped me arrive at this place I am now in the Spirit.

Since meeting them, I've completed two books. One that has been recently published (Before the Throne) and the other I plan on releasing next year. I have more books to come. They helped me to tap into what the Father has put in me, and trust what God has put in me instead of living in fear. Pastor Kisia helped me to walk in a level of faith that I've never walked in that continues to increase because I watched God provide nearly 75% (if not more) of the money for my book to be published. The miracle testimony I have concerning that process is crazy. I am a transformed person. I see myself more through the lens of CHRIST. I see my purpose as vital to the Kingdom. I'm just different. There's so much more I can say but I am grateful to the both of them because not only have they helped me spiritually but they both have shown so much support for my husband, me, and our ministry. There's no pretense in them and in the process of my book coming out they thought it not robbery to promote it and encourage others to buy it. They're different, and I thank GOD for the honor to know them both. To me they are mentors, parents in the LORD, encouragers, correctors and all that. They've helped me and I love them sincerely for it. I know this is long, Prophet, but this is my heart towards you both. You just don't know. Bless you both.

~**Prophetess Jamila Jordan Moody**

*Thoroughbreds, I charge you to **prophesy**, **decree** and **declare the Word of Lord!***

www.ingramcontent.com/pod-product-compliance
Lightning Source LLC
Chambersburg PA
CBHW052035070526
44584CB00016B/2045